W9-AVK-504

ALL ABOUT LIVING IN HAWAII

Norvelle Sannebeck

ALL ABOUT LIVING IN HAWAII

Pacific Books, Publishers
Palo Alto, California

Maps pages 10, 142, 166, 182, 198 by James A. Bier. Photos pages 16, 22, 38, 46, 54, 80, 90, 98, 108, 116, 122, 220, 226 courtesy Hawaii Visitors Bureau. Photo page 68 by Richard Dawson.

LIBRARY OF CONGRESS CATALOGING IN PUBLICATION DATA

Sannebeck, Norvelle.
    All about living in Hawaii.

    Bibliography: p.
    1. Hawaii—Description and travel—1951-
—Guide-books. I. Title.
DU622.S25   996.9'04   77-23732
ISBN 0-87015-224-6

PACIFIC BOOKS, PUBLISHERS
P.O. Box 558, Palo Alto, California 94302, U.S.A.

Preface

As everyone in Hawaii knows, Mainlanders are those unfortunate people who live in Passaic, Portland (either one), San
Diego, or San Whatever—with Canadians thrown in for good
measure.

This book was written for the millions of Mainlanders who are
planning or thinking or dreaming of living in Hawaii sooner or
later, temporarily, seasonally, or permanently.

The aim is to help them make up their minds, to facilitate the
transition of those who do move to Hawaii, and to help new
residents to live happily in the Aloha State.

The book is based on a concept I introduced in a book I wrote
a few years ago about living in Mexico: questionnaires from
residents—in this case from a cross section of Mainlanders now
living in Hawaii. As you read the candid, often amusing, sometimes conflicting answers to the questions commonly asked of
those who have moved here, you'll learn the pros and cons of
living in Hawaii.

Kindly regard the statistics and prices mentioned only as
general indicators—time and inflation move fast. And please
forgive what may be familiar. Who hasn't been to Hawaii, at
least via the TV screen?

Finally, my heartfelt thanks to the hundreds of residents of
Hawaii who, in effect, wrote much of this book through their
helpful answers to my written and oral questions. Theirs was
truly the aloha spirit.

And special thanks to the staffs of the Hawaii Visitors Bureau, Chambers of Commerce, libraries, local newspapers, and
the Department of Planning and Economic Development.
Their assistance and advice were invaluable.

NORVELLE SANNEBECK

Contents

Preface   5

**PART I: QUESTIONS (AND ANSWERS)
ABOUT LIVING IN HAWAII**

1. Why Do Thousands Move to Hawaii Every Year?   11
2. What Do New Residents Think of the Climate and
   the Insularity?   17
3. What Has Hawaii Got Besides Palm Trees and
   Ukeleles?   23
4. What Is Good and What Is Bad About
   Living in Hawaii?   39
5. How Do Residents Spend Their Leisure?   47
6. Does the Mixture of Races and Cultures Cause
   Problems?   55
7. Is the Cost of Living Really That High?   69
8. How Can One Best Manage Money and Household?   81
9. What About Jobs and Business Opportunities?   91
10. What About Young People and Schools?   99
11. Is Hawaii a Good Place for Retirement?   109
12. Do You Have to Learn the Hawaiian Language?   117
13. What Do They Eat There That's Different?   123

PART II: HAWAII'S MAJOR ISLANDS

14. Oahu: The Gathering Place   143
15. Hawaii: The Big Island   167
16. Kauai: The Garden Island   183
17. Maui: The Valley Island   199

PART III: THE DECISION TO MOVE TO HAWAII

18. Making the Decision   221
19. Tips for Newcomers   227
    Suggestions for Further Reading   235

PART

QUESTIONS (AND ANSWERS)
ABOUT LIVING IN HAWAII

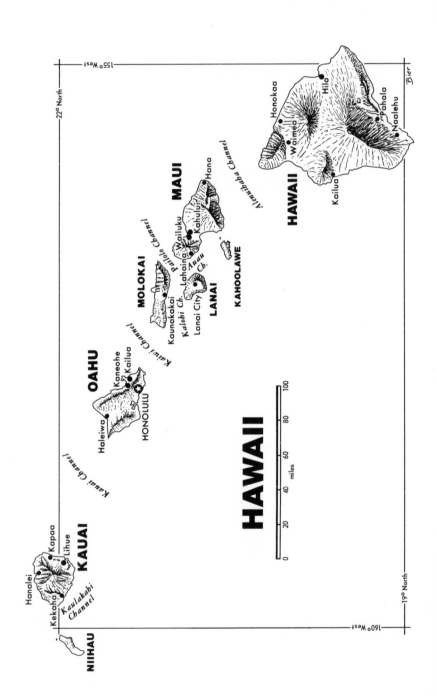

1

Why Do Thousands Move to Hawaii Every Year?

The *real* reason I moved to the Islands is because I was offered a job that paid $15 a week more than the one I had on the Mainland. But who wants to hear a dull story like that?—Bob Krauss in his book, *Here's Hawaii.*

Bob Krauss moved here from South Dakota in 1951 to become a reporter for the *Honolulu Advertiser,* and he is still writing for the *Advertiser.* I dare say he has written more Hawaiian lore than any man alive except James A. Michener, who moved here to write his epic book *Hawaii,* which anyone with an iota of interest in Hawaii should read.

I, too, came here to write—to write this book. At least that was my excuse. Actually I had longed to live in Hawaii since 1954, when my wife, Melva, and I spent two idyllic weeks in Waikiki on our way home from a diplomatic assignment in India.

That wasn't my first visit. While serving in the Marine Corps during World War II, I was transferred from Samoa to Majuro. I flew to Oahu to await onward transportation by ship. Upon being told I might have to wait for weeks, I was elated. I rushed to the then-as-now pleasant Moana Hotel, quaffed a planter's punch, and got on the waiting list for a room. But by nightfall, despite my hopes, I was flying toward Majuro.

In 1960, on my third visit, I was luckier. As a member of President Eisenhower's entourage (I was still in the diplomatic service), I enjoyed the luxurious hospitality of Henry Kaiser's then new hotel, the Hawaiian Village. Currently a member of the Hilton chain, this 20-acre, 1,736-room (at last count) complex is so big that it offers guided tours.

Except for brief in-transit stops, I didn't get back to Hawaii
again until the seventies. Meantime I had retired from the
diplomatic service (at the age of 51), and my wife and I had
moved to Mexico. After we had lived there several years I
wrote a book entitled *Everything You Ever Wanted To Know
About Living in Mexico.*

Wherever we live, Melva and I get restless for a change. She
says that if I ever get to heaven, they'll have to clip my wings to
keep me there. Small wonder that, after the birth pangs of the
Mexico book subsided, we took off for Honolulu to ponder
writing a book on living in Hawaii, one that we hoped would be
not only informative, but also fun to write and to read.

In Honolulu I talked with a cross section of residents: jour-
nalists (Bob Krauss among them), teachers, students, industri-
alists, retirees, and military personnel (15 percent of Hawaii's
population is military).

Almost universally they agreed that Hawaii-minded Mainlanders (the term in Hawaii for residents of continental United
States and Canada) and newcomers to Hawaii need a book to
acquaint them with what it is really like to live—not just tour—
here. The few dissenters feared that the pros of living in Hawaii
would so outweigh the cons as to encourage a host of interlopers
(as they themselves once had been) to flock to the Islands.

Next I drew up a questionnaire similar to the one I had used in
preparing my Mexico book. Then my wife and I lived for brief
periods in housekeeping apartments on each of the major islands. We talked to hundreds of people and distributed questionnaires to representative Mainlanders who had moved to
Hawaii. Additional questionnaires were distributed through
cooperating Chambers of Commerce, the Hawaii Visitors Bureau, and other kind, middlemen.

I digested my preliminary material during a trip to Mexico and
a freighter cruise through the Micronesian Islands. Then we
returned to Hawaii for an indefinite period to collect more
questionnaires and other material and to write this book.

Now let me tell you about the thousands of Mainlanders who
come to Hawaii.

How many Mainlanders dream of living in Hawaii temporarily, seasonally, or permanently? Not even the census-takers know. But statisticians calculate that in recent years an average of more than 40,000 have come annually with the intention of living here.

What types of Mainlanders come here to live? The military accounts for the biggest chunk of the annual migration. Then come professionals, technicians, businessmen, and students. Retirees trail the field, possibly because of Hawaii's reputation as an expensive place to live (more about that later).

Where do they hail from? Three out of five come from the West Coast. The largest number come from California. Migrants from California are known as Coast *haoles—haole* meaning Caucasian. The term is sometimes used deprecatingly because, deservedly or not, Californians have acquired a reputation for wanting to change Hawaii into a miniature California. Next in numbers are Washingtonians, then Texans.

The majority of newcomers head for the island of Oahu, at least at first. Most of the remainder head for one of the other three major islands.

Most of the newcomers are comparatively young. Half are under 24 years of age, owing largely to the number of students and military dependents.

A special statistic for the ladies: incoming males outnumber females by 20 percent. (And never-married males in Hawaii greatly outnumber never-married females.)

Now let's turn to the questionnaires and see what influenced my pollees to move to Hawaii.

I asked "Was your move dictated by job or job offer?" Two out of five answered *Yes.* The number would have been higher if my poll had not included housewives, students, self-employed people, retirees, etc. Of those who came because of jobs or job offers, I'll wager that many, military and civilian, *wangled transfers* to Hawaii. And, of course, the acceptability of many jobs was enhanced by anticipation of pleasurable Hawaiian living.

Pollees whose moves were not dictated by job or job offer were asked to check all applicable items on a list of five common move-influencers and to write in others.

Here are the percentages who checked the listed influences:

Seeking better climate	78%
Seeking less congestion	70%
Seeking slower pace	66%
Seeking better recreational facilities	40%
Seeking employment	15%

Here are samples of the write-ins. (Some of the quotations here and elsewhere I have edited for brevity and clarity.)

"Desire to see more of the world—someplace different."

"Absence of poison oak and snakes."

"Girl friend was here."

"We like the tropics and wanted an informal but cosmopolitan area."

"Too much smog in area where we had lived."

"The racial make-up and the different ethnic cultures here."

"Seeking adventure."

"I was tired of rushing around 24 hours a day."

"Hawaii is a new frontier."

"The beauty of the islands."

"Too cold on Mainland in winter—too hot in summer."

"A good place to raise kids and get away from the Mainland race tension."

"I wanted to leave the husband I then had."

"Love for a girl and for Hawaii."

"Hated Texas—loved Hawaii during frequent visits."

"Just came over—fell in love with the place and people and stayed!"

"Getting married to a longtime resident."

"I got this far on my yacht *Mañana* and abandoned a world cruise." (He plans to stay permanently.)

"Sixty to eighty-five degrees every day" (formerly in investment business, Detroit).

"Desire to be outdoors the year 'round. Love of nature."

"I married an island boy" (and now has two children and plans to stay "Always").

"I moved here under the guidance of the Lord" (formerly a teacher in Illinois).

"The fact that papayas grow in Hawaii" (an expert on papayas, formerly of California).

"The climate agreed with my arthritis" (former rancher from Montana).

"Our love of the people here and the friendliness and beauty everywhere."

"Utter insanity and a desperate lack of purpose." (This beautiful young lady appears to be utterly sane and happy in Hawaii.)

"Violence on Mainland."

"Running away from my problems." (Two years later she operates a private school and seems well adjusted.)

"Romance of the islands. Both my grandmother and my mother wanted to come" (home economist from Colorado).

"Love of the islands and their way of life."

"I came on a visit and stayed. After arrival from L.A. I was drunk on fresh air for a week."

"A chance to never be cold again" (formerly of Seattle).

"Gracious living—no smog, no rat race, no traffic." (She doesn't live in *Honolulu*.)

"Desire to experience the mystique of Hawaii."

"Divorce proceedings."

"My commander suggested it would be good for my career to take this command."

Now you know some of the reasons why Mainlanders move to Hawaii and what they seek here. What do they actually find? We'll get into that in the next chapter, which deals with that big move-influencer, climate.

What Do New Residents Think of the Climate and the Insularity?

> Owing to constant trade winds which blow over the group, cooled by an ocean current flowing from the Arctic, the climate is milder and different from that of most tropical countries.—*The Hawaiian Guide Book,* 1875.

"How about the climate?" That is a question frequently asked of *kamaianas* (long-time residents) by Mainlanders, many of whom have misconceptions about Hawaii's climate.

Some hear of or experience a spell of hot, humid weather at Waikiki, perhaps with frequent rain, and accept the myth that such weather is typical.

The truth is that, because of geographical differences, no one kind of climate is typical. Let me explain.

Contrary to the belief of some Mainlanders, not everyone lives on the island of Oahu, where Honolulu (and Waikiki) are located. Many live on the islands of Hawaii (which confusingly bears the same name as the state), Kauai, Maui, Molokai, and Lanai (known as the Neighbor Islands).

Climate varies according to location. The state can boast of mountains that tower close to 14,000 feet, the highest lake in the United States, a waterfall with a 1,750-foot cascade. Snow skiing as well as water skiing is a popular winter sport, although the snow is unpredictable.

Mountains account largely for wide variations of rainfall. Here's what happens. Hawaii is cooled during most of the year by balmy tradewinds blowing from the northeast. Those winds have crossed a lot of water and are saturated with it. The mountains bend the wind upward to cooler altitudes, forcing the release of moisture. The areas southwest of mountains normally are the driest, because the moisture has been sapped from the winds when they reach the leeward side. Some leeward areas are as dry as the Sahara; others, like the Honolulu area, get pleasant showers because the mountains crossed by the tradewinds are not very high. And there are still other explanations, too complicated to go into here, for other geographical variations in rainfall.

The leeward areas get rain mostly in the winter when the wind sometimes reverses direction, bringing so-called Kona storms. At other times the winds die and temperatures rise—to cause what is called Kona weather, which can be uncomfortable in some places.

I should perhaps explain that the "windward side" of an island isn't a place where winds rage. It means simply that the tradewinds come from that side, the northeast one.

Now let's get down to examples and figures. Would you believe that the highest temperature ever recorded in Waikiki was 93°? In downtown Honolulu, 88°? And that a five-minute drive from either place will take you up several hundred feet and down several degrees of temperature?

As·to rainfall, contrast Honolulu's shoreline annual average of 22 inches with Seattle's 39 inches and Miami's 60 inches.

Suppose I give you the temperatures and precipitation in heavily populated areas (at principal sea-level airports) of the major islands. Bear in mind that, in each case, many people live nearby at higher altitudes and lower temperatures.

Average Temperature

CITY	JAN.	APR.	JUL.	OCT.
Honolulu (Oahu)	72	74	79	78
Hilo (Hawaii)	71	72	75	75
Kona (Hawaii)	72	74	77	77
Lihue (Kauai)	71	72	78	77
Kahului (Maui)	72	73	78	77

Note the contrasting rainfall in Hilo and Kona, the main residential areas of the island of Hawaii.

Average Precipitation

CITY	JAN.	APR.	JUL.	OCT.	ANNUAL
Honolulu (Oahu)	3.8	1.3	.4	1.8	22
Hilo (Hawaii)	11.8	11.9	9.8	10.8	137
Kona (Hawaii)	3.1	1.6	2.5	1.7	25
Lihue (Kauai)	5.5	3.3	1.9	4.0	43
Kahului (Maui)	3.1	1.4	.4	.9	16

For comparison here is similar information for some representative Mainland cities:

Average Temperature

CITY	JAN.	APR.	JUL.	OCT.
San Diego	55	62	70	66
San Francisco	51	56	59	61
Seattle-Tacoma	38	49	65	52
Miami	67	74	82	78
Houston	54	69	83	71

Average Precipitation

CITY	JAN.	APR.	JUL.	OCT.	ANNUAL
San Diego	2.0	.8	–	.5	11
San Francisco	4.0	1.3	–	.7	19
Seattle-Tacoma	5.7	2.4	.8	.4	39
Miami	2.0	3.9	6.8	8.2	60
Houston	3.8	3.2	4.3	3.8	46

I'm not especially good at analyzing that kind of information but a few striking things catch my eye.

The temperature spread between January and July is much greater in all of the Mainland cities than in the Hawaiian cities.

All of the January temperatures in the Mainland cities are lower than those in the Hawaiian cities.

July temperatures in Miami and Houston are higher than in any of the Hawaiian cities.

In summary, it appears that one is more likely to find a warm climate with only minor variations in temperature in Hawaii

than on the Mainland. Only in the mountains does the temperature drop to freezing or anywhere near it. The warm climate
suits many people, particularly the elderly. On the other hand, if
you enjoy drastic seasonal changes, lots of snow, and unpredictable weather, as some do, the Hawaiian climate might
not suit you, although many Hawaiian houses do have fireplaces or other means of heat. Why else would there be in
Honolulu a store called Fireplace-Hawaii, which features pre-
fabricated fireplaces and fireplace accessories?

The Chamber of Commerce says, "One of Hawaii's chief
assets is her mild and temperate climate, relatively free of
uncomfortable extremes." I have found few residents who
would quarrel with that statement.

Pollees had almost universal praise for the weather, tempered
by scattered complaints about too much dryness in Kona and
Kihei. Other residents in both of those areas said that they
especially like the dryness.

As for too much rain, the only complaint came from Hilo, by
far the wettest city in the state.

One pollee (I was surprised there weren't more) said the thing
she likes least about living in Hawaii is the lack of change in
climate. Formerly a Dallas resident, she said, "I do like four
seasons."

And now that we've disposed of weather as a move-influencer
and topic of conversation, we can move along and dispose of the
myth that islanders, particularly those who have moved here
from the Mainland, suffer from claustrophobia owing to the
limited area—which for all islands combined is less than that of
New Jersey.

I was a firm believer in that myth when I asked on my questionnaire, "Do you feel cooped up by the relatively limited land
area?" To my surprise, when I tallied the replies I found that
only about one out of every twenty answered *Yes*. Many of the
negative answers were emphatic, e.g., "Absolutely not!"

At the suggestion of an official of the Hawaiian government, I
added to my questionnaire the following: "Do the mountains
and expanses of water give you a feeling of spaciousness?" On
the basis of his twenty-eight years of residence in Hawaii, he

expected a host of affirmative replies to this question. I didn't. I was wrong. Only one out of every fifty said that they fail to get a feeling of spaciousness from the mountains and expanses of water. A few made qualified replies such as *Yes & No, Possibly,* and *Not on Oahu,* but the overwhelming majority replied affirmatively, many with emphasis.

Since preparing my questionnaire, I have had the pleasure of living at various localities on the islands of Oahu, Hawaii, Kauai, and Maui. I bisected, trisected, and otherwise dissected those islands during the preparation of this book. I can truthfully say that I have joined the vast majority. I, too, do not feel cooped up in Hawaii; the mountains and expanses of water give me an invigorating, satisfying feeling of spaciousness.

What Has Hawaii Got Besides Palm Trees and Ukeleles?

Hawaii is not the tropical paradise that it is made out to be.—Russell Leonard, who moved from Michigan to Hawaii in 1965.

A delightful land to settle in. Most places are what you make them—it's just a little easier in Hawaii.— Mrs. Sheila Hassell, retired businesswoman who moved from British Columbia to Hawaii in 1962.

Hawaii has countless palm trees and ukeleles, all right, but neither is native to these islands. Polynesians brought the palm trees; Portuguese introduced the ukelele (and the Hawaiian or "steel" guitar).

What's Hawaii got besides palm trees and ukeleles? It has people, more than 800,000 of them, and more pineapples than people, a billion at a time. It has Waikiki, the most famous resort in the world—but you already know that.

Let me mention some less-publicized things that Hawaii hasn't got. For instance, billboards, snow shovels, poison oak and poison ivy. Many folks will tell you that Hawaii has no snakes, but don't believe it. I'll explain later.

And let me mention a few things that are scarce in Hawaii. Smog, for one, and heavy traffic, except in the Honolulu area. And unpleasant weather. And ill-natured people. And the frenzied pace of the Mainland.

And now some facts and features about this unique state that should go a long way toward answering the common question, "What is Hawaii really like?"

FROM CANOES TO CONDOMINIUMS

The third inauguration of Governor John A. Burns, which I was privileged to attend, could have happened only in Hawaii.

Some five thousand of us sat on folding chairs under the shade of gigantic banyan trees in the park adjoining Iolani Palace, the only royal palace in America.

The Governor and his retinue strolled over from the Palace and took their places in the old bandstand constructed for the coronation of Kalakaua, Hawaii's last king. Invocations and speeches were brief. Don Ho, Hawaii's singing idol, backed up by a mixed chorus, closed the program.

Following the ceremony, the official party walked to the magnificent Capitol building nearby, followed by thousands like me to attend the public reception. While drinking orange pop, munching a ham sandwich, and enjoying the Hawaiian music of a choral group, I meditated on the history of Hawaii—from canoes to condominiums.

Historians say that Hawaii was first settled sometime between 500 and 1,000 A.D. by Polynesians who came from Tahiti or from the Marquesas in double-hulled sailing canoes.

The first discoverer from the western world was British Captain James Cook, who landed on Oahu in 1778. He called his discovery the Sandwich Islands, after the Earl of Sandwich.

The first chief to unite the islands under one rule was Kamehameha. The Kingdom of Hawaii, which he established in 1810, existed until 1893.

Captain Cook was followed by whalers and traders in sandalwood. American missionaries from New England arrived in 1820, bringing calico from which they fashioned *muumuus* (technically, *holokus*) to clothe the half-naked women, much to the disgust of visiting sailors.

The Kamehameha dynasty ended with the death of Kamehameha V in 1872, and the election of a king by the legislature. The last Hawaiian monarch was Queen Liliuokalani, who was deposed in 1893. A provisional government converted Hawaii into a republic in 1894.

In 1898, with the outbreak of the Spanish-American War, the United States yielded to the pressures of annexationists and annexed Hawaii. In 1900 it became a Territory. Demands for statehood went unanswered for sixty years, but at last Hawaii became the 50th state on August 21, 1959.

So much for history—this is a book about today and tomorrow. Besides, too many good writers have written already about Hawaii's history. If you wish to delve further, you may do so in some of the books described in the Suggestions for Further Reading in the back of this book.

LIFE AND THE LAND

The history of Hawaii has always been linked to the land.

Hawaii is composed almost entirely of eight islands. Ninety-eight percent of the land is on the six largest mentioned earlier. The seventh, Niihau, is owned by one family, the Robinsons; the eighth, Kahoolawe, which is barren, is used exclusively for military purposes.

In the middle of the last century, the land in the kingdom was divided up by King Kamehameha III. Most privately owned land soon came into the hands of a few descendents of the early missionaries and traders. The picture hasn't changed much today. Forty-two percent of the land is controlled by the state, county, and federal governments. Fewer than 100 individuals, corporations, and trusts own an additional 46 percent. That doesn't leave much for anybody else.

The large landholders have always been loath to sell. They prefer a system called leasehold, which means that if you want land for a house, farm, or factory, you will probably have to lease it for a long term, usually 55 years, with a substantial down payment and with the rent fixed for only the first 30 years, after which it will be renegotiated. Lessees pay the taxes, may sell the leases and may make improvements and remove them upon termination of the lease. What usually happens is that lessees don't remove improvements; they simply renew the leases at higher rents. As one of my pollees said, in speaking of leased land for housing, "The buyer must get accustomed to the idea that in all likelihood he will not be here long enough to see his lease run out, therefore why worry."

Only about 156,000 acres (less than four percent) of the land on the six major islands is designated for urban use. Unfortunately, much of that land is vacant and not on the market for prospective homeowners.

Owing to the limited quantities of land available for housing, the high cost of transporting building materials to Hawaii, and the avariciousness of many landowners, speculators, developers, contractors, and suppliers, home-seekers with middle and low incomes are disadvantaged, to put it mildly. The government has been giving urgent attention to the housing problem, with some success. I'll tell you more about housing in Chapter 7, which deals with the cost of living.

SUGAR, PINEAPPLE, NUTS, AND SUCH

Every schoolboy learns, or is supposed to learn, that Hawaii grows a lot of sugar and pineapple. His geography book may tell him that Hawaiian sugar amounts to about one-fifth of world production. It may not tell him that the average American citizen eats more than three pounds of pineapple a year and that around two pounds of that comes from Hawaii. Recent economic reports would tell him that the Hawaiian pineapple industry is being phased out because of its inability to provide technological advances to offset high labor costs.

I guess I'm an above-average American, because I probably eat more than three pounds of pineapple a *month* when I'm in Hawaii, not to mention too many pounds of delicious (but expensive and fattening) Hawaiian-grown macadamia nuts.

The canoes of the Polynesians were heaped, so the historians tell us, not only with dogs, fowl, and pigs, but also with coconuts, slips from breadfruit trees, bananas, sugar cane, and taro, from which that Hawaiian staple food, poi, is made. The historians are not sure about how and when pineapple got to Hawaii, but as early as 1813 it was recorded as growing wild in this sunny climate. A funny thing about pineapple: it's a fruit but doesn't grow on a tree.

Other fruits now grown commercially in Hawaii are bananas, passion fruit, oranges, tangerines, avocados, guavas, mangoes, lichees, and papayas. A special word about the papaya: the people here who are promoting the Mainland marketing of this golden delight tell me that one papaya contains three times as much vitamin C as an orange, and half of one has no more calories than half a grapefruit. If you haven't tried a papaya that has been spiced and baked, you're in a culinary rut.

Other important crops are coffee, vegetables, seeds, melons, flowers, ornamental plants, and those macadamia nuts I mentioned. Everyone from Hollywood's Jimmy Stewart to Hilo cab drivers has invested in macadamia groves.

Unless you're a vegetarian, you'll be glad to know that Hawaii produces good beef: enough to supply about half of the local market; enough to ensure a supply for the growing number of good (and inexpensive) broil-your-own steak houses.

Agriculture's chief problem is common to all sectors of the Hawaiian economy—competition for land, labor, and capital—and its unwelcome result, rising costs. To this must be added inefficient marketing and promotion of most products, as well as inadequate development of new products. But Hawaiians aren't sitting under palm trees brooding about those problems. In 1970 a State Agricultural Development Plan was completed, and its implementation begun.

MILLING AROUND AND MAKING OUT

If you think Hawaii's economy is strictly agricultural, or that its manufacturing is largely limited to sugar milling and making little chunks out of big pineapples (as it was not long ago), let me bring you up to date.

There's a lot of milling around Hawaii. In addition to sugar mills, there are sawmills, steel mills, and flour mills. As for manufacturing, Hawaii is not only making out with pineapple canneries, but also with oil refineries, cement plants, chemical plants, food processing plants, garment factories, and handicraft shops.

Location and lack of raw materials have been a handicap, but since Hawaii became a state, the increase in volume and diversity of local manufacturers has been startling. In spite of gains in manufacturing, Hawaii still imports most of its consumables. As manufacturing increases, imports (distressingly subject to the dictates of dockworkers) may diminish and prices drop.

THE FORCE OF THE ARMED FORCES

Oahu is headquarters for United States defense in the Pacific area. The military is a big force in Hawaii, not only numerically but economically. Its impact may be measured by an annual defense expenditure of approximately $800 million—by far the major source of income to Hawaii.

Some residents, irked by the military contribution to Oahu traffic and competition for scarce housing, wish the military presence would go away. But to the 30,000 or so civilians who work for the military and the countless suppliers of its commodities and services, the military forces are most welcome. Military expenditures for consumer goods, notwithstanding heavy patronage of commissaries and post exchanges, are the delight of retailers. And the military helps not only the economy but also the ecology: the military bases consistently outdo civilian areas in disposal of wastes and beautification of housing and work areas.

THE HUSTLING VISITOR INDUSTRY

In Mexico, tourism is called the industry without chimneys. In Hawaiian trade circles it is known as the visitor industry. Call it what you like, it rivals the military as a source of income for Hawaii. About two and a half million visitors stay overnight or longer each year, leaving behind about $900 million.

The presence of tourists in Hawaii, like the military, is inevitable, and their absence unthinkable. The visitor industry is hustling in the sense of the word that means *energetic, speedy.* (So speedy that there is a superabundance of high-rise hotels defacing Waikiki.) Occasionally I hear complaints that the industry habitually hustles the visitor in the same sense of the word that means *to obtain money in questionable ways,* but this is not borne out by a visitor reaction survey conducted by the Hawaii Visitors Bureau. I'm going to set down here some of the visitors' ratings because residents as well as visitors use the facilities surveyed.

| | *Hotels* | | | |
	OAHU	HAWAII	KAUAI	MAUI
Excellent	45%	46%	44%	51%
Above-average	26	26	29	26
Average	24	20	20	16
Below-average	4	5	5	4
Poor	1	3	2	3

For the following facilities, the survey lumped the islands of Hawaii, Kauai, and Maui together as the Neighbor Islands.

Restaurants

	OAHU	NEIGHBOR ISLANDS
Excellent	39%	31%
Above-average	33	34
Average	26	32
Below-average	2	3
Poor	1−	1−

Shops and Stores

	OAHU	NEIGHBOR ISLANDS
Excellent	33%	26%
Above-average	36	33
Average	30	38
Below-average	1−	2
Poor	1−	1−

Golf

	OAHU	NEIGHBOR ISLANDS
Excellent	40%	61%
Above-average	31	26
Average	25	11
Below-average	3	2
Poor	1	1−

Beaches

	OAHU	NEIGHBOR ISLANDS
Excellent	58%	57%
Above-average	25	26
Average	13	12
Below-average	3	3
Poor	1	2

Fishing

	OAHU	NEIGHBOR ISLANDS
Excellent	33%	36%
Above-average	30	30
Average	29	25
Below-average	5	5
Poor	3	4

HAWAII'S LARGEST EMPLOYER

Not the sugar plantations, not the visitor industry, but the government (federal, state, and county) is Hawaii's largest employer. The government employs one out of four members of the work force.

Apologists say that more branches and more manpower are needed, because Hawaii is made up of so many islands. Others explain that Hawaii as a young state had a lot of catching up to do to bring it up to the standards of other states. Some officials make no apology, saying that the Hawaiian government does more than most others—is more responsive to the public needs. There is substantial evidence to support this view.

One thing the taxpayers agree on: they're glad that Hawaii is unique among the states in having only two levels of government. There are no municipal governments. The only administrative units in addition to the state are the counties of Hawaii, Kauai, Maui (which includes the islands of Molokai and Lanai), and the county (and city) of Honolulu, which administers the island of Oahu and some minor islands.

TODAY'S DRUMBEAT

The Polynesians communicated by drumbeat. Today only the drumbeatings of public relations men and women and of musicians are heard in the land.

Communication is now by telephone, radio, television, and the printed word. Hawaii at my last count had more than 30 radio stations, 5 TV stations, and 7 daily newspapers. Because satellite-relaying is expensive, many television programs in Hawaii have been taped and flown here for showing after their Mainland showing dates. Cable television is now authorized for all of Oahu and is spreading fast on the other islands.

Telephoning is not expensive. Calling from anywhere to anywhere on any one island is a local call—no long distance charge. The price of inter-island calls starts at sixty cents for a station-to-station call at night. And direct-dial calls to the Mainland start at $1.80 for the seven westernmost states.

GETTING THERE AND EVERYWHERE

Almost all passenger travel *to* Hawaii is by air. You can fly from various Mainland cities on your choice of seven or eight airlines, each dangling various traveling treats to attract trade. Fares are cheap, and you can get some island-hopping included for a few dollars a hop. Ask your travel agent for details. The fare structures are so complicated and changeable that even he may be confused. I admit I am.

Although Hawaii is the most isolated heavily populated area of the world, in flying time it is close to any Mainland city, because 747's and DC-10's fly between the West Coast and Hawaii in about five hours. For any readers who are timid about flying, I might add that air travel is far safer than car travel, or for that matter, bicycle travel.

If you prefer to travel by sea, ask your travel agent about the fine ships that sail between the West Coast and Hawaii. I've even made the trip by freighter, and so can you.

Getting around *on* the islands is mostly by private or rental car. There are more autos per capita here than in any other state. Except for Oahu (notably Honolulu), bus transportation is negligible. Traffic is heavy in Honolulu and some other parts of Oahu, especially during rush hours. On the Neighbor Islands, congestion is the exception. As to accidents, Hawaii has its share, although most drivers are courteous and efficient (some will dispute me on the latter). Unfortunately, in Hawaii as elsewhere many drivers are drunk, particularly at night.

Travel *among* the islands is largely by two local airlines, Aloha and Hawaiian Air. One airline would suffice and permit more economical operations, but a merger remains elusive. Commuter service is provided by small planes of small airlines, sometimes operating from small airports. There are military and senior citizen standby fares and off-hour rates.

Inter-island freight, for the most part, goes by regularly scheduled barge service. An inter-island hydrofoil line for passengers was inaugurated in June, 1975.

THE ECONOMY YESTERDAY, TODAY, AND TOMORROW

I've touched on some aspects of Hawaii's economy. Now I'd like to add a few summary remarks.

One thing sure, as goes the nation, so goes the state—with qualifications arising from Hawaii's insular position and its singular dependence upon tourism and the military.

A major problem, one that Hawaii is facing up to, results from the laissez-faire growth of the 1960's, of which the over-development of Waikiki and the spawning of poorly planned housing developments are prime examples. Now with reaction setting in from ecology-minded residents, some of whom are opposed to *any* economic development, there is tough sledding in Hawaii (to use a ridiculous figure of speech) for all development. As a former president of the Hawaii Visitors Bureau has said:

Now it is fashionable to disregard the economic part of our life altogether, and we have come to the point where all development is bad development. This one-sidedness in our thinking will probably serve us as poorly as did our earlier preoccupation with only the economic side of life. Particularly at a time when we recognize the expanding need for parks, sewage disposal systems, good educational opportunities, and all the other things which government does, there must be revenue. Only a viable economy can produce that revenue.

There you have it, the battle of a decade: the economy vs. ecology. The ending will not please the extremists of either side; let's hope it will be reasonably satisfactory to the masses in the middle.

THE CULTURAL COSMOS

Oriental, Polynesian, and Western influences intermingle in Hawaii to provide a unique cultural environment that is diversified yet harmonious—one of the islands' most attractive features.

Music. Who hasn't heard the pleasant strains of *Sweet Leilani, Lovely Hula Hands,* and *To You Sweetheart, Aloha?* Or the comic lyrics of *The Cockeyed Mayor of Kaunakakai* and *Little Grass Shack?* Did you know that there is no mayor of Kaunakakai? And that *Little Grass Shack* is a parody on a long-forgotten song of the 1930's called *My Little Black Shack in Hackensack, New Jersey?* Did you know that those songs were all written in the 1930's? *Sweet Leilani* was written in an hour by band leader Harry Owens as a lullaby for his daughter. It won an Oscar as the best movie song of the year when Bing Crosby sang it in the 1937 motion picture *Waikiki Wedding.*

Pure Hawaiian music consisted only of chants, rhythmic but without harmony. The coming of the missionary hymns was followed by the melodies of Charles King and other Hawaiians. Queen Liliuokalani wrote *Aloha Oe (Farewell to Thee),* plagiarizing the tune from an old hymn. Finally, modern songs such as those mentioned above and more recent melodies have been written mostly by local non-Hawaiians or part-Hawaiians.

Dance. The hula, like a woman, needs no eulogy. It speaks for itself, for the movements of the hands tell the story. Hawaii's unique contribution to the arts, which started as a sacred dance, is seen today mostly in bastardized versions not necessarily less enjoyable to watch than the old-time hulas.

Visual Arts. Early Hawaiian art took two forms: rock drawings (petroglyphs) and sculptured wooden images of the gods. Both reflect the close link between the ancient Hawaiians and nature. The petroglyphs, if done today, would be called abstractions and praised for their stark simplicity. The sacred carvings are the pride not only of Honolulu's Bishop Museum but also of the British Museum as well. (I won't go into modern Hawaiian art here, but will give it some attention later.)

Crafts. I'll do no more than list a few of the ancient crafts, examples of which can be viewed at the Bishop Museum, the Polynesian Cultural Center, and in Ulu Mau Village on Oahu: canoe carving, pandanus plant weaving, lei-making, featherwork, tapa pounding (tapa is a paper-like cloth made from bark).

I know of no place in the world today that is more conscious of crafts, old and new, than Hawaii. The new crafts and variations of the old Hawaiian ones can be seen in numerous stores and galleries, some of which I'll mention later.

Attire. Missionaries, Orientals, and hippies all have made a mark on Hawaii's attire. Missionaries brought the body-concealing Mother Hubbard, made more attractive by the Hawaiians, who added styling and called it a *muumuu* (pronounce each *u* separately). Modern variations, some of which are body-revealing, continue to be the style in Hawaii. Pleasing to me is the custom among business women of wearing muumuus to work on Fridays.

From Japan came the most common footwear worn in Hawaii, thong sandals called zori.

Longhaired transients who don't go barefoot have adopted the *zori* as their own. Transient females are almost as likely to be seen in a *muumuu* as in their more common uniform of tattered jeans or short shorts. Many transients of both sexes are in accord with a habit of the Hawaiian ancients—going without clothing. Some islanders see this as a bad thing, but I'm told that doctors say the closer your skin temperature is to the weather temperature, the better you'll function physically.

Almost everyone in Hawaii today, like the Hawaiians of old, seems to have an aversion to wearing shoes. On my wife's first visit, she and I were entertained at luncheon downtown by a lawyer friend wearing a suit and tie. After lunch we went to his car for a sightseeing trip. Before starting the motor he removed his shoes and socks. Then he drove barefoot. We were surprised but have long since learned that this is a common practice among adults.

Shoes are not always worn to school by children in the lower grades. Football players kick the ball barefoot. Shoes are taken off upon entering the homes not only of the Japanese but also of many occidental ex-Mainlanders as well. In some theatres and restaurants shoes are required wear; in escalators they are required for safety reasons. In such cases the requirement is prominently posted.

Aloha Week. Oahu's biggest annual festival is Aloha Week, dedicated to fun the Hawaiian way. It is held each October, when the number of visitors is low, and some people have been heard to say that the sole purpose of Aloha Week is to remedy that situation. But defenders of Aloha Week look upon it as an opportunity to pay homage to the Hawaii of yesteryear, while casting aside for a time the cares of today. Aloha Week is marked by balls, parades, contests, and costumes. The *muumuu* is worn everywhere by almost every girl and woman of Hawaiian ancestry. A king and queen are crowned and feted. The festival has been described, rightly, I think, as an island Mardi Gras.

RUNDOWN ON RELIGION

Hawaii's religions are as diverse as its churches. Religions include almost every old-line Protestant sect one could name as well as; Catholic, Mormon, Jewish, Quaker, Buddhist, Taoist. The Metropolitan Community Church is primarily for homosexuals. Striking church buildings include what is said to be the smallest Catholic church, a tiny, wooden, metal-roofed building on the island of Hawaii that wouldn't seat a good-sized choir; the imposing St. Andrew's Cathedral in Honolulu, of British stone and Gothic architecture; the Kawaiahao Church, also in Honolulu, which was built in 1841 of coral blocks contributed by members and served as the royal chapel; and the Prince of Peace Lutheran Church that sits on the 12th floor atop Laniolu, a retirement home in Waikiki.

Information about religious activities may be obtained from the Hawaii Council of Churches, 200 North Vineyard Boulevard, Honolulu, Hawaii 96817.

THE DOGBITE AND SNAKEBITE BIT

If you should be so unfortunate as to be bitten by a dog in Hawaii, you needn't worry about rabies; it doesn't exist here. If you go hiking, no need to worry about poison oak or ivy. You won't encounter any. But if you know what to look for, you can gather herbs and plants to make teas that my wife and a multitude of others swear have marvelous medicinal properties.

The only place you can get a snakebite is in the zoo. Elsewhere Hawaii is free of snakes, unless you want to get technical and count the *typhlops braminus* as a snake. No more than six inches long, blind, and biteless—to unscientific types like me, they're worms.

Hawaii is also free of malaria, Rocky Mountain spotted fever, and smallpox, but not of VD.

The health department, created by royal edict in 1850, is the oldest in the United States. Hawaii has more than 30 hospitals, the majority of which are accredited by the American Hospital Association. I won't bother you with statistics on the numbers of doctors, dentists, and nurses. They're in short supply, of course, but Mainlanders should be accustomed to that.

Perhaps I should also add a footnote about abortions. Hawaii was the first state to liberalize abortion laws. Abortions are permitted on request.

WRAP-UP

One might say that there are really three Hawaiis. There is the workaday Hawaii of Honolulu, much like a Mainland city, but more colorful. California detractors call it Glendale with tradewinds—and move there by the thousands. Then there is Waikiki, the seaside playland that needs no further elaboration here. And finally, there are the villages and rural areas of Oahu and the Neighbor Islands, still much like the Hawaii of yesteryear.

Hawaii is plainly no paradise. Like all of its sister states, it has economic, social, and political problems galore.

Along with those problems, Hawaii has a benign climate, a not-so-rush-rush pace, a near-smogless sky, fabulous beaches, gorgeous scenery, exceptional recreation facilities, generally a lack of congestion, and (almost uniformly) friendly, courteous people.

What Is Good and What Is Bad About Living in Hawaii?

> There are advantages and disadvantages to living anyplace. I feel we have more of the former and less of the latter. I don't plan to leave.—Mrs. Harold Toda, formerly of Oakland.

My questionnaire asked: "What do you like *best* about living in Hawaii?" and "What do you like *least* about living in Hawaii?"

In general the *likes* were much the same as the factors that influenced the move to Hawaii. Climate was almost universally mentioned, and many references were made to people, pace, absence of smog and congestion (in most places), scenery, flowers, friendliness, beaches, other recreational facilities, informality, etc. It would be repetitious to quote more than a fraction of the *like bests,* but I think you will enjoy and profit by reading some. Please bear in mind that some comments I quote here and elsewhere represent minority opinions.

"Cultural uniqueness."

"The local philosophy of living."

"Multi-racial spirit of aloha."

"Climate, recreation, but mainly less violence than on Mainland."

"Relaxed atmosphere, the weather, and the people."

"Absence of race violence (that is, for the present)."

"Away from most of the tensions and bad living conditions of U. S. Mainland."

"Meeting people from other States and countries and the native Hawaiians."

"Inter-racial harmony—while not perfect—is far ahead of U. S. Mainland."

"Less changes in temperature, friendly people; I even like the growth."

"Guests from the Mainland who come to share the beauty of our island."

"I admire the local customs."

"Suits, ties, coats are incongruous here."

"Relaxed pace of living, climate, beauty of nature, friend-liness of people" (Ken and Diane Sanders, formerly of Tib-uron, California, now owner-operators of The Foundry, an outstanding art gallery in Honolulu).

"Balmy climate, greenery, flowers, water sports, art and cultural institutions, people's smiles" (Dorothy Klopp, Air Force housewife).

"The gentleness of the people and weather."

"The ocean, the flowers, the mountains, the youth of the islands, virgin land, friendliness of people" (Annette Mc-Williams, retired teacher from Phoenix).

"All races living together peaceably."

"The spiritual atmosphere, simplicity, beauty, lack of pre-tense in all things."

"Climate, slower pace, lack of air pollution, lack of con-gestion, scenery, variation of geography" (Hugh Townsley, physician, formerly of Ohio).

"Lack of formality in associations and dress."

"There are so many things it's impossible to select one! People! Climate! Scenery! Fresh air! But people best!" (from Seattle).

"The oriental and Hawaiian people: their beautiful attitudes and willingness to learn about others and help others" (Bonnie Tuell, home economist, from Brighton, Colorado, who moved to Hawaii in 1958).

"No riots yet!"

"Beautiful skies with many interesting cloud formations, and colorful sunrise and sunset tints, plus the inspiration of the mountains with beautiful views and a chance to cool off, and the many pleasures that the ocean has to offer."

"The high ratio of unmarried men to women" (Signed "Still hopeful").

"Appreciation of things other than money as life's goal."

"Beach parties are always memorable experiences."

"The good natured easygoing customs and people."

"Fewer ridiculous questionnaires to answer."

Now I'll give more or less equal space to dislikes. To the question, "What do you like *least* about living in Hawaii?", the most common answer, by far, was "The high cost of living." Here is a sampling of replies:

"Difficulty in buying what you want."

"The hippies and transients that live off the land but don't contribute to it."

"Racial prejudice." (I'll cover this in a later chapter.)

"Provincialism—aversion to most ideas that are 'new.' "

"Too many tourists and hippies."

"Distance from the Mainland."

"Congestion on Oahu. The other islands are great."

"In some cases the problem of Haoles with Orientals concerning young people."

"It's the second most expensive State." (Alaska is first.)

"The politicians."

"My landlord."

"High cost of inter-island transportation."

"The stranglehold of the Big Five."

"The cost of living is outrageous!"

"Distance from my grandchildren and old friends, although most come sooner or later."

"Lack of 'world' awareness."

"High cost of gasoline and housing."

"Finding housing."

"Lack of places to go and high cost of entertainment."

"The thought of dying."

"High taxes and leftish politicians."

"Professional isolation" (an architect).

"Too much loyalty to ethnic groups."

"The prospect of its getting more congested."

"Low grade of education!"

"Traffic in downtown Honolulu."

"People who come here and complain about my islands." (Ten years sure make a person possessive.)

"Rust and mildew."

"People who complain about Hawaii as a whole but seldom if ever leave Oahu."

"Nothing. It's ideal."

"Difficulty of shopping and getting repairs."

"Too many new developments and greedy promoters."

"Pollution and the unconcern for natural resources."

"Hippies and chippies are a festering sore in Paradise."

"The inevitable racial prejudices."

"I like BIG cities."

"Kona wind."

"My typewriter was to have been ready today after repairs. The shop just called and said there would be a week's delay." (Thanks for the call, anyway.)

"The cane fires." (She lives in the midst of canefields.)

"The transient population."

"Being labeled as a *haole*."

"Tourist gouging, hippies, high gas price."

"The lack of comprehensive zoning to protect the environment from being devastated."

"Being far away from family."

"Schools." (I'll cover this in a later chapter.)

"The growing crime rate."

"I could name a list of pests in Paradise: rats, fruit flies, queers, etc."

"The slow pace here appropriately called 'Hawaiian Time' is frustrating to one accustomed to rapid accomplishment."

"Inadequate highway signs."

"The population explosion."

"Abandoned cars. Why not collect them and recycle them into machines for collecting and crushing them?"

"Fireworks!"

"Needless horn blowing."

"Bugs." (One professor says that if population and pollution keep growing we may end up eating bugs—so maybe this fellow is just ahead of his time.")

The *like bests* above speak pretty much for themselves, but comment may be in order here about three of the major *like leasts:* crime, irresponsible transients from the Mainland, and pollution.

To find out how residents are affected by crime in Hawaii, I asked my pollees "Do you worry much about personal safety or security of property?" The answers may surprise you; they did me.

Ninety percent of the pollees on the Neighbor Islands said they don't worry much. On Oahu, more crowded and Mainland-influenced, the non-worriers were fewer—50 percent. I wonder what a similar poll would show in Mainland areas.

Here are some illustrative comments:

FROM OAHU

"Mainlanders have taught locals all the tricks of crime."

"We need more police and tougher judges."

"I don't go out alone at night" (lady from Los Angeles).

"I don't feel safe to be out at night" (another lady in Waikiki).

"Too many burglars."

"Judges are too lenient."

"Vandalism and housebreaking are increasing."

"Our apartment has been entered twice."

"We didn't move 3500 miles to be hung up on personal property."

"This is one of my hang-ups, but I feel it less here."

"Traffic is a concern, crime not especially."

"Open living is conducive to robbery." (Sadly true!)

"Laws are too lenient. Police do not investigate to fullest extent."

"There is a great deal of drug-induced and juvenile crime."

"Can leave my home unlocked without worry" (a minority view on Oahu).

FROM HAWAII

"No one has to worry here."

"We have had our place robbed twice."

"We have two Dalmatians, mansized."

"Changing for worse as Mainland influence comes."

"I've worried only since the hippies have come."

"It's the safest place in the world."

"Perhaps I should worry, there's a bullet-hole in my window."

"In the area where I live houses are unlocked" (A not uncommon practice in many areas of the Neighbor Islands).

FROM KAUAI

"I worry less than I would anywhere else in the world."
"No need to worry."
"Since the hippy element has come we do lock our doors."
"Haven't locked the house in five years."
"Complete trust—never lock doors."
"Not too much crime here yet."
"The hippie influence makes me worry."

FROM MAUI

"I only hope the relatively secure feeling can last."
"Don't even lock my house."
"I lived a year and a half in a house with no doors we could lock."
"I don't have to worry as I know the Lord Jesus Christ."
"Hippies have not discovered us yet!"
"We do have to lock up now because of the undesirables coming from the Mainland."
"Least worry of anywhere I've been."
"I've never mistrusted anyone here."
"This is the first place I haven't been afraid alone at night" (lady from Seattle).
"I worry about the influx of transients with drug addiction."
"Our house was burglarized a few months ago, but only a few coins were taken."

Consider the dilemma of the man who wrote me, "We should have a watchdog but my wife is allergic to dog hair." He may find consolation in the knowledge that if someone in his household should be the victim of assault and battery, murder, or rape, the state government might make monetary apology, despite the contributory factor of his wife's allergy. The State Criminal Injuries Commission regularly makes compensatory awards to crime victims and their families.

I hope and look for improvement in the crime picture. Bur some people don't seem much concerned. Take the New York woman who during a three-week visit had her hotel room burglarized, had articles stolen from her rented car, and finally was mugged in Waikiki and relieved of her valuables. She still thinks Hawaii is a great place to visit. "The climate and scenery," said she, "outweigh what has happened to me."

Though part of the crime is attributed to gangsters who have imported their methods into the islands, a large part is attributed to the so-called hippies. I call them irresponsible young transients, who come in search of sexual adventure, slothfulness, and drugs (not necessarily in that order). All of those things cost money, and a drug addict will go to almost any extreme, short of working, when in need of drugs.

Naturally, many irresponsible transients are on welfare rolls, despite restrictive legislation passed in 1974. As one resident put it, "They take advantage of our tax dollar through the welfare system." Another said, "Transients who are on the welfare rolls are getting away with the biggest con job in the world."

Small wonder that underfinanced visitors, with their contribution to crime and welfare rolls, are not liked in Hawaii.

Growing like the crime rate is a wave of complaint and resentment against the despoilers of the landscape and the polluters of air and water. The rising voices of the ecology-minded are beginning to be heard and heeded in the halls of government, local, state, and federal. That is good for Hawaii, which still is relatively free of blight.

So much for likes and dislikes. Now I'll close this chapter with the words of a fellow who advises against living here:

"It's a great place to visit but not to live—now that I'm here I don't want anyone else to come" (A former Alaskan).

How Do Residents
Spend Their Leisure?

So many things to do that there aren't enough hours in the day to do everything.—Sam Arginteanu, senior citizen pharmacist, formerly of Miami Beach.

In any sunny resort-type area, visitors frequently ask residents what on earth they find to keep them busy. A popular misconception is that residents spend most of their spare time snoozing under a palm tree for want of something more stimulating to occupy their bodies and minds.

For most people who have moved from the Mainland to Hawaii, the problem isn't how to keep busy; it is how to find time enough for all the things they would like to do.

What things? Well, in the first place, they continue to do most of the things they did on the Mainland. In addition, Hawaii offers a variety of sports, recreations, and entertainments far beyond what is found in most places on the Mainland, at least on a year-round basis. Hawaii also offers unique cultural attractions and novel opportunities for stimulating civic and social work.

Outdoor recreational activities figure so largely in the lives of most residents that I turned for detailed information to a comprehensive survey made by the state. In what activity do you think the highest percentage of residents participate? Swimming? No, but you're close. Swimming ranks second. Here's the rundown of sports:

Pleasure driving, sightseeing	69%
Swimming	68
Playing outdoor sports, games	56

Picnicking	54
Sunbathing	44
Walking for pleasure	42
Motorcycling, bicycling	37
Attending sports and cultural events	35
Surfing	32
Scuba, skin diving	26
Fishing	23
Boating	21
Golf	14
Hiking	11
Shooting	9
Camping	6
Horseback riding	6
Hunting	5
Water skiing	4

A few footnotes of my own may be in order:

1. I would add to the list beachcombing for shells and coral, running and jogging, beer drinking, backyard barbecuing and luauing, people-watching—of girls especially, and skiing on snow (sometimes) on the island of Hawaii.

2. Fishing is mostly in the ocean and mostly for marlin (billfish), yellowfin tuna, dolphin, swordfish, bonefish. There are no seasons, no limits on catch, no salt-water fishing licenses.

3. A survey of Oahu came up with the amazing (to me) conclusion that 10 percent of that island's population spends 165 hours each year, or one month of full-time "work" in surfing.

4. Hunting is mostly of deer, wild goat, wild pig, wild sheep, pheasant, partridge, quail, dove. Hunting regulations are as generous as license fees are nominal.

5. Spectator sports include professional baseball, football, and tennis, and college football as well.

6. Hawaii has nearly fifty golf courses, most of which are open to the public, and annually hosts a PGA tourney, the Hawaiian Open.

7. Public facilities for tennis and camping are mostly free.

For entertainment, Hawaii offers a unique calendar of events. Here is a list (subject to change) of some of the major ones. These events are on Oahu, unless otherwise noted.

JANUARY

Hula Bowl Football Game. East-West All-Stars.
Narcissus Festival. Chinese New Year festivities. A major celebration in Honolulu. (Continues into February.)

FEBRUARY

Haleiwa Sea Spree. Water sports galore on Oahu's north shore.
Hawaiian Open Invitational Golf Tournament.
Ski Meet. On snow-capped Mauna Kea, island of Hawaii.

MARCH

Cherry Blossom Festival. The Japanese try to top the Chinese festivities. A major celebration in Honolulu. (May continue into April.)
Easter Sunrise Services. At Punchbowl National Cemetery. (May fall in April.)
Kamehameha Schools Song Contest.

APRIL

Buddha Day. Festivities on all islands, highlighted by festival in Honolulu.
Hawaiian Music Festival. High school competitors from Hawaii and the Mainland.

MAY

Lei Day. Everybody wears a lei. Festivities on all islands, particularly at Waikiki.

JUNE

Kamehameha Day. A state holiday honoring King Kamehameha the Great. Statewide festivities center in Honolulu.

JULY

International Billfish Tournament. At Kailua-Kona, Hawaii. One of the world's top fishing events.

AUGUST

Hula Festival. Sundays at Kapiolani Park Bandstand, Waikiki.

Duke Kahanamoku Memorial Canoe Race. From Lanai to Waikiki.

SEPTEMBER

Waikiki Rough Water Swim. All ages and categories.

OCTOBER

Orchid Show. Orchids, bonsai, cactus, and flower arrangements.

Aloha Week. Major activities on Oahu with related festivities on other islands.

County Fairs. At Kahului, Maui and Hilo, Hawaii.

NOVEMBER

Duke Kahanamoku Surfing Classic. On the north shore of Oahu.

DECEMBER

Festival of Trees. Elaborate exhibits of decorated Christmas trees and Yule items for sale to benefit Queen's Hospital. Not to be missed! Christmas carols by choral groups.

International Surfing Championships. The surfing classic of the world.

And now let's turn to my survey of the activities of residents, excluding work, which is a major occupation of many. This is how my pollees answered the question "How do you spend your time mostly?"

Frequently mentioned were many sports, outdoor recreations, and other common activities such as gardening, loafing, reading, television-watching, entertaining, painting, and community affairs. I'll give you just a few replies that cover a wide range of activities.

"Promoting the study of Spanish."

"Senior Citizen activities."

"AAU swim official for teenage swimming clubs."

"Trying to stay outdoors as much as possible."

"Driving around seeing new places."

"Living graciously, entertaining neighbors at dinners, picnics on beach, shelling, museum and library boards, etc."

"So much to do here—so much beauty."

"State Commission on Aging, American Association of Retired Persons, Senior Citizens Action Club, Hawaii Yacht Club, Adventurers Club, etc., etc." (Arthur Pawlison, former Boy Scout executive from Bellingham, Washington. Age 75+).

"Concerts in the parks and taking a Bible correspondence course."

"Flight instructing is my hobby" (electronics engineer from Sacramento).

"Not much change from Mainland—slower pace is nice."

"Flying and singalong parties" (former Colorado rancher).

"Entertaining visitors. A timetable for visitors should be sent to Mainland friends each year" (Claude Wardell, formerly of Santa Barbara).

"Working with Teen Challenge, an organization that helps young drug addicts."

"Kill time at the hotels."

"Horizontal."

"We have many interesting and pleasant times with Hawaiian friends at their parties and luaus."

"Learning the cultures of all the races in the islands can keep one busy" (Retired nurse from Pittsburgh).

"I act as an extra in *Hawaii Five-O,* which is most interesting."

"Life could be humdrum—but we are active in community functions; also we grow our own vegetables and most fruits. We play considerable golf, spend a lot of time on the beach. Meeting and living with the local peoples, especially the non-Caucasians, has been educational, exciting, humorous at times, but never distressing" (Andrew Hammond, formerly of Seattle).

"I'm a member of the Consular Corps, the American Association of Retired Persons, the Caledonian Society, and am a part-time employee of a travel agency" (age 65+).

Now I'll close this chapter with three comments that illustrate some of Hawaii's exceptional leisure-time opportunities.

First a list of some activities given me by Mrs. Tom Leuteneker, a housewife, who used to be an elementary school teacher in California.

1. Ti-leaf sliding.
2. Sailing at sunset on Hilo Bay with a pitcher of mai tais.
3. Spotting whales off the beach and watching them frolic.
4. Listening to my son's nursery school class sing Hawaiian and Tahitian songs (with motions).
5. Watching a shark hunt.
6. Seeing a volcano erupt at night and listening to the roar—while choking on sulfur fumes.
7. Digging up a Kalua pig for a luau.
8. Jeep riding on the lookout for wild peacocks.

Ti-leaf sliding, in case you don't know, is tobogganing down a muddy hillside on leaves from the ti plant. (Whiskey is made in Hawaii from the roots of this plant.) An even more curious sport engaged in by young and old in Hawaii is fluming. This is floating on your back down a mountainside irrigation ditch.

Mai Tais are the unofficial drink of the state of Hawaii. Secret recipes are rife. A later chapter will deal with food and drink, but I can't keep my secret recipe until then.

Top Secret Mai Tai (Double)

1 measure (you pick the size) of light rum
2 measures of dark rum (you pick the type)
1 measure of pineapple juice
½ measure of lime or lemon juice
½ measure of your favorite orange liqueur
    A few drops (be careful, it's strong) of
        almond extract—or use orgeat syrup, if
        available.

Mix and pour over crushed ice into two glasses, the prettier the better. Garnish with whatever you have that looks exotic. If you don't have orchids, settle for pineapple sticks or mint. Share with your wife or some other pretty girl.

Mrs. Leuteneker wasn't by any means the only pollee to mention volcano-watching. Here are some observations by Frank Drees, who came here in 1923 from Urbana, Illinois.

Hawaii is in its infancy, geologically. The active volcano creates new land almost continuously on the island of Hawaii, but the whole island chain, extending along the so-called Northwest-Southeast rift is still in the formative stage. Volcanic activity in Hawaii is unique in that whenever an eruption is mentioned in the news, young and old by the thousands flock to the scene of activity. I have watched many flows and eruptions and am still awed and inspired by the mighty forces of nature that have created these beautiful mountains and lands of lava, cinders, and ash. The National Parks on Hawaii and Maui offer truly some of the most remarkable geological scenery in the world. Once you have stood beside a molten lava river, you will never forget the adventure.

My final comment comes from Marianne Bullock, a librarian formerly of San Diego, now of Pukalani, Maui.

I enjoy spending time at the beach and being accepted by groups of local (very mixed) people to share their food, drink, music, dancing, talk-story, and general fun. This happens all the time. Also going camping with our church group, all Japanese but me. Also hiking through and camping in the Haleakala crater with a mixed group.

I thoroughly enjoy island life and think anyone would who is willing to join in the way things are done here. There's always more to do than one has time for. You can live the leisurely life or be as active as you choose.

And so you see that in Hawaii one need not spend his time snoozing under a palm tree, although I recommend a little of it now and then. But let me caution you not to sleep under a coconut. They've been known to fall and break up both nap and noggin.

Does the Mixture of Races and Cultures Cause Problems?

Haoles, Hawaiians, Japanese, all mixing together at parties, church, service clubs, etc. proves that we have a common bond. When peoples of all cultures, colors, and status can live together as they do in Hawaii, it is proof to the Mainland and the world that mankind has a chance to survive if one can get to know his neighbors.—L. M. "Jack" Prince, formerly of Los Angeles.

Not the least of the problems facing the Territorial Legislature when Hawaii was about to become the 50th state was that of selecting an official "popular" name for the new state—a nickname. Suggestions included the Pineapple State, the Sugar State, the Sunshine State, etc.

The final selection was the Aloha State. What could be more apt? Aloha is a Hawaiian word (now anglicized) meaning, according to its context, greeting, love, welcome, farewell, compassion, affection. It has come to be symbolic of the way of life in Hawaii that stems from the ancient communal attitudes and customs. To the people of Hawaii it signifies mutual respect, assistance, and harmony among all.

Aloha was well defined by the Reverend Dr. Abraham Akaka, a Chinese-Hawaiian, at a service of thanksgiving for the admission of Hawaii to statehood:

Aloha consists of a new attitude of heart, above negativism and legalism. It is the unconditional desire to promote the true good of other people in a friendly spirit, out of a sense of kinship. Aloha seeks to do good to a person, with no conditions attached. We do not do good only to those who do good to us. A person who has the spirit of aloha loves even when the love is not returned.

A writer for a local newspaper says that the old feelings of aloha are passing. "They still exist here and there among close friends who lived through the 'old days,' but the vastly increasing number of strangers coming through Hawaii are making it well nigh impossible to pass the spirit on."

A local anthropologist says:

The whole theme of Hawaii as a homogenized blend of races is a myth. Much of what we've taken pride in about how well the races get along here really has to do with how well we've contained our conflicts by placing constraints on open discrimination. The question is whether this attitude is really healthy. The real problem to face is to make this world safe for genuine diversity.

A contrary view is taken by columnist Sammy Amalu, part-Hawaiian, who says he is born of many bloods. He wrote:

Are we Americans? Or are we not? How long must we remain Japanese, Chinese, Puerto Ricans, Filipinos, Hawaiians, *haoles?* How long must we continue to gauge each other's value by the hue of the skin, the texture of the hair, or the cut of an eye? Are we not yet able to lose our varied ethnic identities in the greater amalgam of our nation and become by long last what we are by national definition: Americans all?

So much for the views of the experts. Let me give you a few personal examples of the aloha spirit.

When my wife and I came here to do the preliminary work on this book, we shuttled from island to island, from family hotel to luxury hotel, from rental Datsun to rental Toyota, from Chinese grocery to modish shops, from Japanese snack bar to Canlis' at Waikiki (by its own admission, "the world's most beautiful restaurant"). Our desire to write this book was heightened immeasurably by the universal friendliness, helpfulness, and courtesy that we encountered from people of all races and walks in life.

Melva's favorite memory of those days is of an experience at a small hotel that offered special rates to military personnel. When I remarked that I didn't suppose the rates applied to me, a military *retiree,* the young desk clerk, a girl of Oriental descent, was indignant. "Why not," she said. "You fought for our country, didn't you?"

The aloha spirit was nicely demonstrated in another hotel by the note left by the maid one morning: "Aloha. Just to let you know the towels will be in later. Mahalo. Judy." (*Mahalo* means thank you.)

We found that the aloha spirit rubbed off on us. I had never had a reputation for being eager to offer my seat to old ladies on the bus, to open store doors for young mothers with children-in-arms, or even to be profuse with such phrases as "Thank you," "You're welcome," "Good morning," or "Good night" to people I meet casually. But following the example almost uniformly set by the islanders (be they natives or johnny-come-recentlies), I found myself, at first by some force of will, later by quickly acquired habit, using such phases unsparingly. One day *the* spirit even moved me to spend half-an-hour getting a car unlocked for a nice tourist from Seattle, who had locked his keys inside. In Seattle I would have let the stupid oaf gain entry by smashing a window, as he had been about to do when I offered my assistance.

What do my pollees think of the people in Hawaii? To find out, I asked them, "Do you find the people here friendly, on the whole?" And I invited comments.

I received only *two* negative replies. All others were in the affirmative, many of them emphatic, only a few qualified. Here are illustrative comments:

"Very much so."

"The friendliest, nicest people anywhere."

"Friendlier here than anywhere."

"We have marvelous neighbors."

"All are friendly if treated so."

"Smiles and willingness to assist in any way possible."

"I find much more friendliness than in New York City where I was born."

"I loved my first experiences with the people here. They were so loving, generous, and helpful—so eager to show us the beauty and wonder of the island."

"We sailed to Hawaii in 1961 in a 40-foot Newporter ketch. On arrival after 16 days at sea the people at Waikiki Yacht Club were very kind to us. We were welcomed sincerely. This introduction to the islands made it very easy for us to return to live 4 years later.''

"I immediately noticed the aloha and friendliness among people."

"99+% are very friendly; too bad it can't be exported elsewhere" (Bud Weisbrud, a friendly young fellow himself).

"Most friendly people I have met anywhere in the world."

"We enjoy genuine friendship with many races" (moved here from Denver in 1963).

"If you are friendly yourself, they most certainly are."

"People for the most part are gentle, kind, and good here."

"There are no strangers if a newcomer is outgoing."

"I've never felt lonely here. I feel surrounded by friends."

"The integration of ethnic groups is wonderful."

"*Kokua* is not just a word here—it is a constant way of living." (*Kokua* means help to others.)

"I have sensed no unfriendliness—have met a great many wonderful people" (written by a wonderful woman).

"Mainlanders must be more sensitive to local culture to prevent tide of resentment."

"Friendly, indeed. I married a local man—the fire chief."

"They are more courteous than people in any part of the U.S."

"The aloha spirit still exists."

Here are some qualifying comments:

"My son has problems in mixing."

"Many seem unfriendly until you prove yourself."

"People are friendliest in country areas and Neighbor Islands."

"Friendly, but prejudiced."

"Adults almost all friendly; teen-age boys not always."

"I find the Orientals more cliquish than any other group."

"There is sometimes an uneasy feeling between locals and whites" (young Oahu beauty operator from California).

"Some anti-*haole* feeling among young people."

"They were very friendly when we first came here 10 years ago but attitudes are changing."

"Some of the locals don't like you because of their stereotype of you."

"People are friendly, but there is definitely subtle discrimination."

"A few sad people still do have color and racial prejudice."

"Friendly, but I find it hard to understand how the locals think."

"The aloha spirit is probably not so strong as formerly."

"At least superficially they're friendly."

Whether the aloha spirit (strong or weak) exists because of Hawaii's multi-racial makeup or despite it, may be debatable. But one thing is sure: everyone in Hawaii is a member of an ethnic minority.

Bear in mind that the census-takers include people in the racial groups of their fathers, as you read the ethnic breakdown:

Caucasian (includes Puerto Ricans)	39%
Japanese	29%
Filipino	12%
Hawaiian	9%
Chinese	7%
Korean	1%
Negro	1%
Others	2%

With regard to the Hawaiians, the state statistician estimates that there were no more than 250,000 at the time of Captain Cook's arrival. He says that pureblood Hawaiians number only a few thousand today. He estimates the number of part-Hawaiians (Hawaiian blood on the side of either parent) at about 130,000 and says that the trend is for them to have less and less Hawaiian blood.

What is the correct way to refer to a resident of Hawaii? As one man has put it, "If all residents of Texas are Texans, of California, Californians, etc., why can't all residents of this state be called Hawaiians?" They can be and sometimes are. In this book, to avoid confusion I try to reserve the term Hawaiian for people with Hawaiian blood.

Mixed ancestry is a common and proud thing in Hawaii. It is said that a quarter of the people are of mixed racial blood. Does the mixture of races make a happy stew? I think so. To supple-

ment my observations, I asked my pollees two questions: First,
"Does the mixture of races and cultures cause *you* serious
problems?"; second, "Does this mixture contribute to your
enjoyment of living here?" I invited comments on both
subjects.

In response to the first question, I received a chorus of *Noes*.
Some answers were emphasized, e.g., "No!" and even
"No!!!" I've selected some examples to show you the general
pattern.

"It's really beautiful the way races and cultures mix."

"I find it very interesting to know other people and find out
something about their cultures."

"Only creates a problem if you make it so."

"Have friends of all races wherever we go."

"One of the best things about Hawaii is total integration."

"One of the delights of Hawaii."

"I love the mixture of ethnic groups."

"No. There are 23 blood lines in my 20 grandchildren."

"Just the opposite."

"I am a *haole*, my husband Japanese. I am accepted by all."

"We all belong to one race—the human race."

"I like people who have *mixed* backgrounds, they are so
understanding."

"My wife is Japanese and we have had no problems" (Navy
officer).

"It is the nicest thing in Hawaii—so educational to be on the
receiving end of prejudice."

"I am not race conscious; I only see individuals as beings."

"We enjoy genuine friendship with many races."

"Anyone is accepted if he is acceptable."

"People should not be all alike. I would greatly miss the
mixture."

"No problem because I adapt to island ways and do not
remain Mainland in my ways."

"I find friends among all the races and mixtures of same."

"That was our main reason for moving here."

"This mingling of races is very good."

"Found one colored couple most helpful—stopped to change
wife's tire."

"I find it quite interesting to study and understand their ways of thinking."

"A model for the world."

"In fact, it helps."

Adverse or qualified comments were in the minority. They included the following:

"Race mixture is healthy with the exception of certain races."

"Not serious problems, but irritation sometimes."

"Mostly the people are quite pleasant. There is a trash element in every society."

"We have found some native Japanese not too receptive to *haoles* coming here to live."

"Communication, particularly between *haole* and Japanese bureaucracy can be difficult."

"No matter what the tourist brochures say about brotherly love here, there is discrimination towards *haoles*. It is subtle, but it is here. I've seen too many unhappy, disillusioned *haoles* go back to the Mainland."

"White people are discriminated against: The races are not as happy together as appears on the surface. (She moved here in 1965.)

"The Oriental population is acutely protective, i.e., one year's residency requirement to practice medicine."

Does the mixture of races and cultures contribute to the enjoyment of living in Hawaii? Here are some typical comments on the subject.

"I enjoy learning of their culture, history, customs, and traditions."

"In our church we have all races and cultures and it's great!"

"It allows us to become familiar with and enjoy many races."

"I've met fine people—gives me a better understanding of other races."

"I have good non-caucasian friends."

"We take advantage of all activities they have to offer."

"From food to life styles, we enjoy them and our son will be better for it."

"Most beautiful people one can imagine." (This man has lived all over the world.)

"I find the intermingling of the various cultures and races fascinating and colorful."

"Definitely. I'm happy to have our children growing up in a mixed culture."

"We enjoy friends of many different races."

"The Mainland is drab by comparison."

"I hope to do my bit to wipe out prejudice."

"It is good to see and learn about other races' way of life."

"Neutral."

"Provides a rich culture—fascinating milieu."

"The mixture adds diversity to what might be too homogeneous otherwise."

"I am learning much about other cultures, customs, foods, etc."

"It is a joy to mix with people of other races and to be accepted."

"I like the many easygoing, non-argumentative, handsome men."

"They enrich your social experience."

"I have many oriental friends."

"Yes, white minority is highly tolerated in most social circles."

"Fun to 'people watch' people with different cultures."

"There is prejudice—but on the whole pretty good acceptance."

"Race stresses seem to be limited to a situation where one or both parties to an argument wish to make it a racial issue."

I received a few negative and qualified replies, such as the following:

"No. Races per se, have never bothered us one way or the other so long as they're nice."

"No. But we have always stayed to ourselves."

"Not especially—I just love to live here."

"No. Don't think about it."

"It would, if it was as amicable as most people think."

"Yes. But there is racial discrimination—outsiders are resented."

"Not particularly."

"Neither contributes nor detracts." (He moved here in 1925.)

"The mixture makes no difference; people are as nice to you as you are to them."

"Not really. It was interesting at first, but I find their cultures very similar."

"There exists a subtle discrimination against Caucasians, especially in the Civil Service."

"Some racial tensions do exist, even here."

"A small minority ignore you or give you dirty looks."

"No trouble socially; jobwise there is a problem" (a teacher).

"It causes me problems mostly in communication."

"If there were fewer young *haoles* it would be easier for me. Hippies give all young *haoles* a bad image" (business owner in her mid-twenties).

"No problems except that I can't speak pigeon English."

"*Haoles* in some professions such as education, real estate, and finance are discriminated against. Japanese dominate in politics, education, and Civil Service. Persons requiring a license to do business may find their way barred by technicalities and indifference."

"There is some racial prejudice but it doesn't show very often."

"It is most distressing to try to find work here in the islands. Most of the hotels and businesses are owned or controlled by Japanese. They definitely are race prejudiced. I find most of the people here hate each other's guts but live in tolerance with each other. I am now looking forward to getting to know the Filipinos—I'm fortunate in having some very close friends among the Japanese and Portuguese." (I have permission to use her name but won't.)

"It came as a great surprise to me that there is as much prejudice toward *haoles* as there seems to be. This, however, is therapeutic since it is well to be on the other side of this sort of thing to truly appreciate the Mainland type of injustice. Here it is a much more subtle thing, but it does exist."

Here are two illustrations of discrimination proffered by pollees:

"It is frustrating to get a 'no hab' answer in a store when the article in question is on a shelf behind the clerk, and the attitude seems to be that 'your skin color is not the same as mine and you

can leave without wasting too much time.' It is most fortunate
that this happens only rarely.''

Another man told me of a conversation between him and a
local electrical appliance dealer (Japanese). The conversation
went about like this.

''My electric clothes dryer has broken down. I'd like for you
to fix it.''

''Did you buy it from us?''

''No, it was here when we bought the house.''

''Then we not fix—we only fix what we sell.''

''But it was bought from you by the previous occupant.''

''No matter.''

''Can't your repairman possibly fit it in?''

''He very busy.''

''When?''

''Don't know.''

''You mean you don't want to fix?''

''Yes.''

''All right, forget it; but we won't buy another appliance from
you.''

''O.K.''

My respondent concluded:

''This is quite typical: no competition, no hustle. But I think
things might have been different had I been Japanese. These are
things you finally get adjusted to—but they are hard on a
newcomer.''

And here is the advice given me by a Los Angeleno, formerly
a resident of Hawaii, when he heard I was writing this book.
(My inclusion of this material should quiet any muttering that I
am painting too rosy a picture of the people of Hawaii.)

You had best keep in mind that you are a *haole* and that what you are
doing is really resented. To their mind, who in the hell are you to come
over there and say what is right or wrong with Hawaii? The great
majority of the people born there have never been anywhere else, so it
is not possible for them to make any comparison. They think it is
perfect, which only shows their ignorance.

Another thing, when you lived in Mexico you knew you were a
gringo and that you were in a foreign country. There, I'm sure, you
accepted as a natural thing that you would be looked upon as a foreigner. In Hawaii, even though it is the U.S.A. you are looked upon as
some kind of second-class citizen unless you were born there and in

effect, a foreigner. The only difference between Mexico and Hawaii in this respect is that you cannot be kicked out of your own country, although in the past and to some extent now, you can be blackballed until you left of your own will. Any kind of opposition to letting your American culture be smothered by the oriental culture of the islands, is to invite difficulties. Even if you fight the political and prejudiced make-up of the local government through the highest courts, they still will not give in and will continue doing as they want to do. You had better point out to prospective immigrants that Hawaii is part of the U.S.A. in name, but in reality it is the orient.

All of Hawaii is a snow job. The biggest pile of crap is this aloha hooey. Too, this business of the golden people living in all this harmony, is something that only the tourists believe. The fact is, inter-racial and inter-nationality friction is as intense there as anywhere I've seen. The Japanese are not in my judgment the most irritating group there. Except for their clannishness and fixed oriental attitudes they are preferable to many other ethnic groups. The worst over there, bar none, are the old time *haoles* and their hangers-on, the ones that were brought over from the Mainland to fill the supervisory jobs in the old days. There is also a type of *haole* who is of recent vintage and who, after a few years (sometimes, even a year), considers him or herself a *kamaaina,* and who is the most obnoxious and anti-Mainland *haole* of them all. You will find them dropping Hawaiian words and expressions on you and shouting aloha to the high heavens. They are usually obsequious to all the natives, especially the Hawaiians or almost-Hawaiians. They really go overboard trying to be Hawaiians in everything and every way.

Now with that lengthy judgment on the record, I'm going to tell you some good things said by pollees about their experiences with local people. Ladies first.

I arrived on Kauai in 1968 and started to work for the newspaper here. In August I met my future husband because I had a stalled car. He passed by on a motorbike and at first glance thought I was a boy and continued on. On his return trip he saw me still trying to fix my car and lo and behold he discovered I was a girl. He stopped and fixed my car and we were married three months later. I'm Italian-Chinese and my husband is Filipino-Portuguese (formerly of New York City).

And now we'll hear, by coincidence, from another New Yorker, now a prominent businessman of Maui, Higgins Maddigan.

When I first came to the islands, I was building a car and met a Japanese man who had been a master wheelwright at Schumman's Carriage. He invited me to dinner many times, where I had the opportunity to meet his three daughters, the eldest for whom marriage had been arranged, the second oldest for whom it had also been arranged (but she did not follow through), and the youngest, who had been allowed to choose her own mate.

During many discussions with the daughters, we had a chance to learn how each of us was raised, our attitudes toward the other race, and upbringing of our families. This was a unique experience in that the *haole* is an enigma to the Japanese, and few *haoles* have the opportunity to learn the Japanese ideas. I consider this the most significant experience, and probably the most useful, I have been privileged to enjoy since coming to the islands.

To Mr. Maddigan's story I would like to add what he told me during a conversation in the striking Lahaina Market Place, of which he is the owner.

Shortly after my arrival in Hawaii, I had financial reverses. One day when I was licking my wounds, a young Chinese friend came to me and offered me $20,000, saying that if I could pay it back later fine, and if not, still fine. I managed to get along without accepting his loan offer that so typified the generosity of the Chinese with whom I have been associated on the islands.

I'll close this chapter with a few stories about deeds that I think typify the aloha spirit of typical islanders.

On a rainy Christmas eve, a young girl knocked at our door and asked for directions to a nearby apartment; we helped her search it out and use our phone. Two hours later, came another knock. It was the girl's boyfriend bringing us a special Christmas gift of fruit, candy, etc. in appreciation for our help.

If you send a *real* Christmas card with a personal check made out to the name of your mail carriers and you should later be a patient in Queens Hospital they will chip in and send you a beautiful floral arrangement with a "round-robin" get-well card signed by "The Boys." In addition they collect your mail and re-route it every day until you telephone the Post Office and tell them the date of your return home. I wondered why I received all this help with my mail. They said, "Most people just throw a dollar bill at you at Christmas, but you take time to get Christmas cards for each of us and mail them to the Post Office with handwritten checks in each person's name." So East and West can and does meet in mutual appreciation!

If you tip your newsboy or mailman at Christmas in what he thinks is an excessive amount, you will find a box of orchids outside your door on Christmas day.

Shortly after we arrived on Maui we had a long walk in the sun to the bank. Apparently we looked warm upon arrival. The teller, to whom we were strangers, invited us to sit down and served us a cool Hawaiian punch. This nice gesture was unexpected and made us feel very welcome. That feeling has never worn off.

I admired a carving that a Hawaiian boy had given my daughter soon after our arrival in Hawaii and remarked I'd like to have one like it. She mentioned the conversation to her friend and next day he arrived with a similar carving and handed it to me. I immediately grabbed my purse and asked the price. He just stood and looked at me for awhile. Then he said "Someday I guess I'll be like you *haoles*—everything for money and nothing for love, but not yet." That was my first lesson in what it really means to live the Hawaiian way.

One day while taking two partial invalids touring, we stopped at the Mormon Temple. There we got into conversation with an elderly Hawaiian lady in a wheelchair, and soon she invited us to her home for tea. By the time we could leave her house three hours later we were laden with mangoes, lichees, pineapple, and a coconut palm hat made for each of us by her grandson. This is the true spirit of Hawaii.

Jean Holmes, editor of *The Garden Press,* Kauai's fine newspaper, told me the following tales.

I came here under the handicap of being a Mainland *haole* placed as a department head over local people. At first, I had trouble making friends and began to wonder if there was something wrong with me, or if 'aloha' was just a fake. After four months of trying to show that I wanted to make friends, and of wondering if I had made any headway, I found a small house to escape to from my over-a-garage apartment. When I told the people in the office about it, lo and behold, they gathered to help me pack, borrowed a truck to move my things, washed the windows, hung the curtains . . . and then cut the grass and trimmed the hedge to give me a good start. I had found the real aloha . . . there when it really counted.

Then last year my doctor decided that I was trying to get pneumonia and stuffed me in the hospital. When I arrived, weak and feverish, the admitting clerk asked the routine question, "Who is your next of kin?" I suddenly had a lone and helpless feeling. Except for my son, fifteen that day, I had no kin in 5,000 miles. I named a neighbor, and was wheeled off to bed, visualizing a lonely death and funeral. Soon my room began to fill with flowers and at visiting hours with the smiling faces of my friends . . . Hawaiian, Chinese, Japanese, Filipino . . . and a few *haoles*! After I came home not a day passed that several friends, of the same fine assortment, did not drop in to visit, always bringing gifts of food so I would not have to cook.

No next of kin? I had next of kin all over this lovely island!

7

Is the Cost of Living Really That High?

In a premium location with a premium climate you pay a justifiable premium to live—A former New Yorker.

No, Virginians—and Californians and Missourians—there is no Santa Claus in Hawaii, as far as the cost of living is concerned. In a nutshell: expenditures for cold weather clothes and heating are almost non-existent for most, but savings on those items are more than offset by high-priced housing, food, cars, and other consumer goods.

Just how much does it cost to live in Hawaii? The answer depends on the size of family, spending habits, type and location of residence, etc., so I can't give you a precise answer. But I will give you a do-it-yourself calculation system based on statistics of the U. S. Department of Labor.

First, an index of comparative costs in representative cities based upon an intermediate level annual budget for a four-person family (employed husband, age 38, wife, 8-year-old girl, and a 13-year-old boy). On this index, 100 represents the U. S. urban average.

Northeast		*South*	
Boston	118	Atlanta	93
Hartford	109	Houston	90
New York	114	Nashville	92
Philadelphia	103	Orlando	90
Pittsburgh	97	Washington, D.C.	103
Non-metropolitan areas	98	Non-metropolitan areas	85

North Central		*West*	
Chicago	105	Denver	96
Dayton	93	Los Angeles	99
St. Louis	98	San Diego	97
Indianapolis	101	San Francisco	106
Milwaukee	105	Seattle	100
Non-metropolitan areas	93	Non-metropolitan areas	90
		HONOLULU	118

The index indicates that, of the cities listed above, Honolulu shares with Boston the highest cost of living, 18 percent higher than the urban average. For consolation, let me add that Anchorage, Alaska, is 31 percent above the urban average.

Comparable up-to-date budgets are not available at this writing for other family patterns. In any event, bearing in mind the constancy of inflation, you should consider all cost of living figures in this book only as general guides. And please bear in mind that costs of newly arrived residents in any given community are likely to be higher.

HOUSING

Most people in Hawaii don't complain much about the weather, but they grumble about the cost of housing with good reason.

I can summarize the situation by quoting from a study prepared for the state government:

> Housing shortages and high prices have been felt especially by the poor and the elderly but also by moderate and middle income households. Residents pay proportionately more of their income for housing than their counterparts on the Mainland.
> The land situation is the largest obstacle facing those attempting to meet local housing problems. While there is certainly no scarcity of land per se, its availability for housing is limited by a combination of factors involving location, concentration of ownership, and public land use and improvement policies. Consequently, the cost of land in Hawaii has been more than three times higher than on the Mainland. Further, the buyer of a home on leased land apparently does not pay proportionately less than on fee simple, even though he gains no equity in the land.

Nearly half of all housing costs relate directly to construction. Nearly all building materials cost more in Hawaii than in Mainland cities as a result of shipping costs, reliance upon wood products, and domination of the building supply industry by a few large suppliers.

Wealthy people can afford to scramble for the high-priced units for sale or rent. The poor have been assisted by government-subsidized housing. Those in between have had a difficult time.

What type of housing may a newcomer expect? He shouldn't expect a little grass shack on a palm-fringed beach. Most one-family houses are one-story, single-wall construction. There are also an increasing number of high and not-so-high apartment buildings. The newer apartments are mostly under condominium ownership, which provides tax advantages, particularly to owners who rent their apartments to others while not in residence.

Some people insist on having air-conditioned living quarters; some prefer to rely on the tradewinds and extensive use of a garden or lanai (porch or balcony). Much of the choice must depend on the individual and the location of the housing. Air conditioning does run up the initial cost of purchase or rent and operating costs.

As to new housing, Mainland trends are setting in. In addition to the condominium pandemonium I have already mentioned, trends are toward pre-cut and factory-built homes, some of innovative design.

I asked pollees who had bought or built their residences to comment on the experience. Here are some comments that reflect a wide range of views.

"Floored by high costs."

"Shocked at prices asked for low quality of construction."

"Took the bank 7 or 8 months to settle the papers but otherwise fine."

"Expensive and difficult."

"We found a good home by answering an ad."

"Took too long and carpentry not the best."

"It's cheaper to buy than to rent on a long term lease."

"The work is not always satisfactory, but that is true everywhere."

"Double the Mainland price for less quality."

"I tried to buy but found the prices ridiculous."

"I'm now building a pre-fabricated home sent from the Mainland—local attitudes make it difficult."

"Bought 4 homes, upgrading each time."

"Very satisfactory experience."

"People tended to take advantage."

"Fantastically inflated real estate situation. A $50,000 leasehold house here equals a $25,000 fee simple one in California."

"Bought an excellent value."

"Very fair treatment."

"We acted as our own contractor. Found material hard to get but saved nearly $2,000."

"Prices much higher here and fee simple land is scarce, but it's worth it to live here."

"You must expect less house and land for your money."

"I bought overpriced homes and now rent them out at overpriced rents."

"We bought a condominium before construction started; 4½ years later the price had doubled."

"We found our house by driving around looking for 'For Sale' signs."

"Prices are high but one can sell even higher."

"We built our own small Armco Steel Company cottage—quite an experience."

"If I had been trying to get rich, I would have bought and built more than I did."

"Bought from local builder—good experience."

"Building is extremely slow."

"It was profitable."

"I have not yet had the courage, having two friends nearly lose their sanity in the process!"

"Everything was fine because we trusted the workmen and left them alone to do their job."

"Choose your contractor very carefully."

"I would buy an older home. The ones built now are junk."

"We built and it was deadly. A $50,000 Mainland house will be double here."

"It's an education in itself to build. Quite a battle for a *haole*."

"Building your own house is enjoyable and rewarding."

"Quality of workmanship below that of San Francisco. Good material is scarce."

"We bought into a condominium and are pleased with apartment living after home ownership for years."

"We chose the land, planned the house, and enjoyed it."

"We four.d building our home a bargain. We got what we wanted for lots less money. Our contractor was good."

How about today's market for home-seekers? The Chamber of Commerce puts it well in two paragraphs of its informative folder, "Living and Working in Hawaii."

For those planning to establish new homes in Hawaii, housing authorities warn that newcomers should be prepared to pay higher rentals than long-term tenants. In the better residential areas of Honolulu, furnished studio apartments rent from $150 a month and up, while a one-bedroom furnished apartment will command $200 or more. The average purchase price for an unfurnished three-bedroom house varies from $50,000 to $75,000. There are no trailer courts or sites for "mobile" homes.

Because of higher land values and more outdoor living, the average family moving to Hawaii lives in a smaller house or apartment than they are accustomed to on the Mainland. You will need less furniture, and major appliances are customarily furnished.

Whenever I'm checking the cost of housing anywhere, I take a look at the local newspaper ads. You can check for yourself by sending 75 cents to *The Sunday Honolulu Star-Bulletin & Advertiser,* P.O. Box 3350, Honolulu, Hawaii 96801 for a single copy.

The cost of utilities is generally comparable to utility costs on the Mainland, with local variations.

Both electric and gas appliances are widely used, although electric are more common. Electricity is supplied by five power companies with varying rates. Manufactured gas is available throughout the state. In some areas piped gas is available; elsewhere bulk cylinder gas is used.

Heating is a minor or non-existent item in most households. It may be provided by electricity, gas, wood, or kerosene.

FOOD

Food takes a big bite from any U.S. budget. In Honolulu the bite is bigger than it is in the average American city because of high transportation costs and weak competition among wholesalers and retailers.

But let me tell you how food prices were *reduced* in Hawaii at a time when they were rising on the Mainland through the use of a technique that, as far as I know, is unique.

In October 1969 the University of Hawaii began a weekly pricing of common items in 25 of Oahu's major food stores, changing the items each week to forestall rigged prices. The listing alone would not have influenced prices, but the Hawaiian government published and distributed 1,000 copies of the two-page report each week. Lowest prices were circled, enabling shoppers to see where items were being offered at the lowest prices. From the reports it was possible, also, to determine how the store ranked in over-all cost of the items.

When storekeepers saw an increasing number of the reports in the hands of shoppers, they were alarmed.

More and more stores gave up trading stamp programs and other promotional giveaways, streamlined operations, and began to buy more in bulk directly from the Mainland. Some of the savings they passed along to their customers. The result: lower prices.

During the first 13 months of this project's operation, food prices on the Mainland increased nearly 4 percent, while prices on Oahu actually decreased at all but four of the surveyed stores. The prices at three stores dropped 9 percent or more. And the weekly reports acted as effective price controllers of food. The reports have been discontinued but may be revived.

TAXES

Taxes are state-administered. There are no county or municipal taxes. Major sources of revenue are the income tax, excise tax, and real property tax. There are no personal property taxes or special local levies for school districts, municipal bonds, and the like.

The income tax follows the federal pattern generally. Personal net income tax rates graduate from 2.25 percent on the first $500 to 11 percent on income in excess of $30,000.

The excise tax rate is 4 percent on retail goods and services, and there is a complementary tax on personal property brought into the state.

Real property tax rates are set by the counties and vary according to land usage. The residential rate per $1,000 valuation is based on 70 percent of fair market value. The rate varies among the islands—all under $20. There is an $8,000 homestead exemption.

Miscellaneous taxes apply to alcoholic beverages, public utilities, motor vehicles (annual license fee), etc.

A summary of taxes levied in Hawaii is available from the Chamber of Commerce of Hawaii, Dillingham Building, Honolulu, Hawaii 96813. Detailed information may be obtained from the Hawaii Department of Taxation, 425 Queen Street, Honolulu, Hawaii 96813.

CLOTHING AND PERSONAL CARE

As already noted, everyone gets a break here from the weather man. Heavy clothing is not needed generally, although some is needed in the highlands of Maui and Hawaii. Many women, of course, like to wear light furs for decoration. In every circle of men there is likely to be one topcoat to be passed around to anyone so unfortunate as to have to go to the Mainland in winter.

Casual wear is commonly worn, although persons traveling in business or high social circles will need some formal attire (and by formal I mean dinner jackets for the men, on occasion, rare though they may be).

Some businessmen still wear suits to work, but the trend is more and more toward Hawaiian sport (called *Aloha*) shirts. These shirts need not be patterned with multi-hued floral designs; conservative colors and patterns are much worn. Shorts can be worn almost anywhere.

For women, apart from the ever-popular *muumuus*, there are (my wife says) *holomuus* (fitted *muumuus*), sunshifts, pant-suits, bikinis, and tunics, often topped by flopping hats.

The cost of this casual attire depends largely on the degree of style and quality desired. The *haute couture* of Hawaii holds an important place in the island economy: fashions are No. 3 among its exports. If you can afford it, when and if you come to Hawaii, leave your old rags behind and get some Hawaiian glad rags here.

"Personal Care" under the Department of Labor scheme of costs is comprised of personal grooming supplies and hair-dressing services. My wife says that she pays no more here than on the Mainland for her tinting, shampooing, manicuring, and whatnot. The same holds true for my haircuts.

TRANSPORTATION

Transportation means cars to most people in Hawaii. On Oahu two out of three go to work by private car; only one out of twenty go by bus. Eighty percent shop by car; 7 percent by bus; 5 percent by walking. Forty-five percent of families have one car; about an equal number have two or more.

A bus network covers Oahu. Service is fair, drivers are courteous, and the fare is 25 cents. There is very little bus transportation on the Neighbor Islands.

There are taxis in all urban areas. On Oahu the price is high. Rates vary on the Neighbor Islands but tend to be lower.

If you bring a currently licensed car from the Mainland, you can get a temporary permit at no charge to operate it until the license expires. (Members of the armed forces may continue to register cars in their home state.)

I won't go into details of Hawaiian car licensing. Information may be obtained from the Division of Licenses, 1455 South Beretania Street, Honolulu, Hawaii 96814.

MEDICAL CARE

A majority of residents of Hawaii are covered by one or the other of two major medical plans: the Hawaii Medical Services Association and the Kaiser Foundation Health Plan.

I am not going to compare the plans here, except to say that Kaiser has its own hospital, clinics, and salaried doctors. It leans heavily on preventive medicine and pays virtually all expenses of hospitalization during the first 150 days per illness or injury each year. Under the HMSA plan, patients have a choice of hospitals and doctors and benefits extend beyond Hawaii. For cost and other details of plans, write to HMSA, 1504 Kapiolani Boulevard, Honolulu, Hawaii 96814, and Kaiser Foundation Health Plan, 1697 Ala Moana, Honolulu, Hawaii 96814.

A dental plan is operated by Hawaii Dental Service, Room 405, 1149 Bethel, Honolulu, Hawaii 96813.

OTHER COSTS

Such things as reading materials, musical instruments, radios, television sets, records, recreations, hobbies, cigarettes, and alcoholic drinks average out at about 5 percent higher than the urban average, although fees and admissions for spectator and participant sports are likely to run less.

The minimum price of alcoholic beverages is controlled by the state. Here are some prices.

Beer (case of 24 12 oz.)	
Budweiser	$6.68
Olympia	$6.28
Primo (locally made, 11 oz.)	$5.96
Whiskey (fifths)	
Johnny Walker scotch, red label	$8.39
Johnny Walker scotch, black label	$11.33
Cutty Sark scotch	$9.39
Old Forester bourbon, 86 proof	$6.79
Gordon's gin	$4.89
Smirnoff vodka	$5.69
Bacardi rum, light	$5.45

Here are some observations of pollees about the cost of living. Almost all of them characterized it as high. Here are some more specific comments.

"High. But so is per capita income."

"Very high, but worth it." (Several people commented similarly.)

"Unprintable." (Some printable comments were "Outrageous," "Hideous," "Unbearable," etc.)

"High, but depends on which level one wishes to live. Luxuries are more expensive."

"High, but not impossible" (a nurse.)

"Higher costs are offset by lesser needs."

"Too high unless you know how to live economically. We fish and pick a lot of fruit." (Her husband is a native.)

"To keep a lawn green and bug free it costs about $10 a month for fertilizer and sprays."

"Very high taxes (too many government employees)."

"Charges are outrageous for appliance repairs, plumbing, etc." (I hear this on the Mainland too.)

"High costs are blamed on freight, but not so. People are getting rich off of us."

"Monopolies to blame."

"People who are unhappy about the prices should never come to Hawaii."

"More truck farms are needed to raise natural foods. We're too dependent on shipping produce in."

"The cost of living is too high but we feel it's worth it to be really living—not 'existing' " (from a couple who know how to get the most out of life.)

"A very large item of expense for us is entertaining friends from the Mainland who 'want to see how you live in Hawaii.' "

"Salaries are not commensurate with the cost of living" (a common complaint.)

"Not bad for most things but housing is rough."

"We grow some of our food and we live simply."

"A little higher than Detroit but better."

"Costs are too high due to lack of competition."

"Too expensive for retired people" (retired shipping clerk who moved here in 1961.)

"Costs are not excessive" (a voice in the wilderness.)

"Costs are lower if you eat differently and don't place too much importance on material things." (She follows her advice.)

"You have to pay through the nose to live in Paradise." (He hails from Hollywood.)

"Two people in a family must work in order to survive."

"In a premium location with a premium climate you pay a justifiable premium to live." (Here I repeat the epigraph with which this chapter began, because it so well expresses the majority view of Hawaiian residents.)

How Can One Best Manage Money and Household?

It's almost an impossibility to economize.—Mrs. Kathleen Ladera, who moved from New York City to Hawaii in 1968.

Householders have the same problems here as on the Mainland, but this is a nicer place to have them. —Jean E. Holmes, formerly of Maryland.

Fully aware of the high cost of living in Hawaii, and hoping for some tips I could pass along to readers and use myself, I asked my pollees, "What are your suggestions on how to economize in Hawaii?"

A number of responses, like that of Mrs. Ladera quoted above, were negative. For example:

"If you have any suggestions, please tell me."

"Someone please tell us all!"

"Wish I had some suggestions."

"I haven't figured it out yet."

"I wish I knew."

"Have not learned to do this during the past 45 years."

Other responses reflected a reconciliation to the high cost of living in Hawaii, for example:

"Don't. Enjoy what nature provides so abundantly." (Mrs. Trumbo and her husband, former Managing Editor, *Los Angeles Times,* have an extraordinarily lovely home and view on Kauai—they know how to enjoy Hawaii.)

"I doubt if it is possible. If you wish to live in Hawaii, you must pay the price for the pleasure." (Dr. W. A. MacDonald lives in a delightful condominium apartment on Maui, where we were once neighbors.)

Pollees offered a variety of miscellaneous advice, for example:

"Eat lots of rice and drink lots of water."

"Same as anywhere—keep within your budget."

"Eat less. Stop buying entertainment. Cut luxuries."

"Don't waste money buying vitamin pills unless your doctor prescribes them."

"Don't buy unnecessary things."

"Buy out of mail order catalogs."

"Learn the annual schedules of seasonal sales and patronize them."

"Shop for second-hand items offered for sale in newspapers, particularly neighborhood and military papers on Oahu."

"Take advantage of free and inexpensive recreational facilities. Beaches, picnics, school programs offer endless opportunities."

"Live close to nature and use what is available."

"Take a step or two down from the way you were accustomed to live on the Mainland."

"Stay out of bars and clubs."

"Don't drink." (Let me add that private label liquors are cheaper than name brands.)

"Eat lightly, shop carefully, and simply make up your mind you will live simply."

"Diet and stop smoking." (Good advice for many of us anywhere.)

"Avoid Waikiki. Eat local fruits and vegetables; drink fruit drinks."

"Minimize long distance phone calls. Own only one car and go no place."

"Learn to eat rice instead of potatoes and become accustomed to local foods."

"Use the lovely free beaches and parks for your recreational facilities."

"Forget a car. Get a bicycle."

"Have a freezer. Buy meat in bulk. Wear shorts and muumuus."

"Turn off unnecessary lights. Order from mail order catalogs."

"Eat seasonal foodstuff."

"Shop every available outlet until you learn where the best values are."

"Don't try to keep up with the Joneses. Life can be as cheap or as expensive as you want to make it."

Now for suggestions relating to items of major expenditures.

HOUSING

"Buy instead of renting."

"Shop carefully for housing not in prime tourist areas, i.e., away from the beaches."

"Don't economize on time when looking for an apartment—there *are* inexpensive apartments available."

"If one can possibly build, the horrible monthly outlay in rent at least goes toward an equity."

"Import lumber from the Mainland."

"Buy a house if you can afford it. You will not sell at a loss and there are tax advantages."

"Rent a crummy house and fix it up rather than renting an expensive apartment."

If you can beat the high cost of housing without living in a tent, you will have scored a major victory in the battle against the high cost of living in Hawaii. Here is one battle plan:

The one way to beat the cost of housing is to become an owner-builder. This, of course, means one must have capital or be able to raise it and be capable of doing the job. Prefabricated houses may be shipped from the Mainland or bought locally. It is quite possible for a handyman in this way to build a house at $10 a square foot or less. In contrast, to have a house built will cost anywhere from $20 to $25 a square foot. [His cost figures are out of date.]

FOOD

My wife priced the following items in four Oahu supermarkets: bread, corn flakes, canned tuna, margarine, eggs, potatoes, tomatoes, peanut butter, mayonnaise, coffee, and canned corn.

She found that the prices for comparable products varied widely. The eleven items if purchased at the highest prices asked would have cost 16% more than if purchased at the lowest prices asked.

I wouldn't suggest that in Hawaii a shopper should run all over town to find the cheapest price on each item. But if you can use a quantity of an item that is an especially good bargain it might be worthwhile to go out of the way to make a bulk purchase.

Now let us pause to see what my respondents had to say about groceries:

"Watch for specials on paper products and economize in their use—they are very expensive."

"Be a vegetarian with your own garden."

"Plant a garden and exchange produce for other items needed."

"Raise animals to eat, have a garden, use fresh rather than canned foods, make own jams from local fruit, bake your own pastries." (Mrs. Tuell on Maui does all this, holds down a responsible job, and takes care of a husband and three children.)

"When you dine out, remember that lunch is much cheaper than dinner at many restaurants."

"Skip paper towels and other bulky items shipped here."

"Take advantage of economical church luaus."

"If you are overweight, get a doctor to put you on a diet and exercise routine to eat less, feel better, and spend less. (It must work—she was slim and healthy and 74 years old when I met her.)

"Get a local boyfriend and have him dive for fish and lobster like I did."

"Learn to like the food eaten by orientals and Hawaiians."

"Learn the locations of wild fruits and how to preserve them."

"Enjoy the good fishing and hunting."

"Eat fish and poi—personally my family doesn't like either."

"Get a freezer and buy beef by the quarter or half."

"Use evaporated and non-fat dry milk instead of fluid milk."
"Eat rice instead of potatoes."
That last comment stems from the high prices of potatoes, which are not grown commercially in Hawaii. Many restaurants include rice with a meal but charge extra for a baked potato. Sometimes there is no extra charge for french fries because, so I'm told, they are imported frozen at less cost per serving than baked potatoes.

For a finale on food costs, I give you the philosophical remarks of one of my correspondents on a Neighbor Island:

> Foodstuffs are generally higher priced than on the Mainland but not unduly so. The main shipping port is Honolulu, so the Neighbor Islands bear the additional charges of shipping from Honolulu. On the other hand, as one becomes more familiar with the area, he may either have such things as bananas, avocados, and citrus fruits growing in his yard, or know friends who have more than they can consume. The climate lessens the requirement for as much food as in a colder area, and shopping at stands that handle off grade items can result in some savings. Island beef may not be quite as tasty as good mid-western cornfed beef, but it can generally be purchased at prices comparable to mainland prices. Frozen meat from Australia may also be less costly, but certain practices apparently of shipping beef and mutton together may give a less desirable taste to the meat that cannot easily be masked.

CLOTHING

"Dress casually."
"Make your own clothes."
"Wear shorts and muumuus."
In Hawaii I wear Aloha shirts, and Melva wears muumuus frequently. She found a way to provide us with an ample wardrobe of those garments at low, low cost. If you're not proud, you can easily follow her example and watch for announcements of church sales and patronize church-operated thrift shops. Can you imagine how many aloha shirts and muumuus are purchased and received as gifts in Hawaii and never worn or maybe worn only once or twice? Racks full, that's how many. Melva once bought me a shirt in perfect condition that had come from Liberty House, a quality store. She knows my taste and size. And she knew the price was right: 15 cents. She has been

known to purchase stylish muumuus of fine materials for little more.

TRANSPORTATION

The cost of motoring comes high in Hawaii, owing to high prices for cars, gas, and repairs. Here are some suggestions for economy:

"Consider leasing a car for a short term rather than renting."

"Shop around when renting. The biggest agencies are often the highest."

"Buy a small car. Drive it for years. Recap the tires." (Distances are short, speedways few, inter-island shipping costs vary with car size.)

"Use car pools for shopping, golfing, and the like."

"Buy your car on the Mainland, ship it yourself, and save money."

Now then let us turn to the subject of householding. My questionnaire asked, "If you run a household, do you find it difficult?" I also asked for comments.

To my surprise, scarcely anyone reported difficulties other than coping with the high cost of living. Here is a sampling of comments on other subjects:

"Domestic help is very hard to get and is expensive."

"Living in an apartment is easy. No household or backyard chores."

"It's hard on me, a widow, to work and keep house for three children."

"Condominium living is almost carefree. Two hours a week cleans the place and that's it."

"This place is so easy going I just take my time and everything always gets done."

"Great need for domestic employment agencies."

"Running a household here is no different than on the Mainland."

"Cleaning and yard help are available."

"I do quite a bit of entertaining—no problems."

"It's no worse than any other place."

The only lengthy comment was the following useful one:

Cockroaches, common in Hawaii, were the only thing unpleasant. Our first apartment was loaded with them. My first few days were frightening. However, my husband equipped me with a bottle of Johnson's *No Roach* and a brush. This helped greatly. I recommend this product for anyone living in Hawaii.

I received several comments about the difficulty of getting minor repair and maintenance work done promptly and economically. Residents of Oahu who are not handy men (or women) can solve that problem by attending the Do-It-Yourself course at the Nuuanu YMCA. The $15 fee can be recouped in savings. Who teaches the course? John Rodrigues, who does all the repair work at the Y, and says he can teach most anyone how to handle tools, change a light switch, make window screens, expand patios, build sidewalks, change toilet parts, and so on.

To my question "Is shopping difficult?" I received a chorus of *Noes*. To my question "Are selections limited?" I received many *Yeses* and qualified answers. Here are some illustrative comments:

"Certain batteries and building materials are hard to find."

"We live simply and camp out a lot, so we don't need a lot of things to select from."

"You can learn to use other products, improvise, or substitute."

"Luxury shopping is difficult and very limited."

"Choice of worldwide merchandise."

"Stores are congested." (She was speaking of the deservedly popular Ala Moana shopping center.)

"Retailers use poor excuse of shipping costs and delays for high prices and low inventories."

"I knew that selections would be limited before I moved here. I accept it."

"Certain items require a tremendous amount of searching to find."

"Markets are well stocked."

"The biggest problem is size selection—almost everything is large."

"Large sizes of clothing are difficult to find; are expensive; also shoddy for the price." (Maybe she and the lady quoted just above should shop together.)

"The point of moving here was not to go shopping; it's easy if you relax."

"A few things are unavailable or frequently out of stock."

"Native foods and clothes are available in small stores."

"Almost everything is available—more so than in Greenville, Texas, for example."

"Shopping is better than I had in Palo Alto."

"Certain items are not restocked right away. Name brands are limited."

"Selections are limited on the Neighbor Islands."

"Clerks not very helpful or courteous." (The only comment of its kind.)

"Many supplies appeal more to the Oriental shopper than to the Caucasian."

"You come to the islands knowing that life is different; why expect all the services and conveniences to follow you?"

"One learns to do without. Often what we had considered necessities are really luxuries."

"You learn to live with the limitations and then it's not difficult to shop."

"We rely heavily on catalog purchasing (Sears)." (So do many others.)

"Items of daily use are readily available."

"We have more supermarkets than are needed."

"Only specialty items are scarce."

"All I need I can find although the selection is limited."

"One learns to substitute and be patient for shipments to come."

"Very limited selection of clothes."

"I would like to be able to buy all organic foods."

"More health foods needed."

"Shopping is fun here."

"Transportation strikes have caused problems."

"I walked into a supermarket and couldn't find the brand of coffee I usually purchased there. Inquiry brought this reply:

'Oh, it sold so fast that we had to re-order so often that we just quit carrying it.' "

So much for what my pollees say about shopping. May I add a few personal observations?

If you come to Hawaii to live, it's odds on that you'll live on Oahu, at least at first. In any event, you'll do a lot of shopping on Oahu because, let's be frank, shopping facilities there are far superior to those on the Neighbor Islands. So I suggest that early in your stay you get acquainted with the major stores and shopping centers of Oahu.

One thing you'll find in alluring variety to attract your spending money is Hawaiian-made gift items for friends, relatives, and yourself—one more thing that runs up the cost of living for most newcomers. These gift items include fashions and fragrant perfumes, jewelry of indigenous and imported materials, exotic flowers and plants, arts and handicrafts of wood, ceramic, lava rock, feathers, and so forth, and tropical fruits and nuts.

No matter where you shop or what you shop for in Hawaii, you have some good consumer protection laws and the Office of Consumer Protection going for you.

The laws regulate such things as advertising, installment sales, solicitation by telephone, charitable solicitations, housing rental agencies, and even escort agencies.

Details of those laws are contained in the booklet *Consumer Protection Laws*. To obtain this booklet and other consumer protection educational materials, or to file a complaint, write the Office of Consumer Protection, Room 602, Kamamalu Building, 250 South King Street, Honolulu, Hawaii 96811.

What About Jobs and Business Opportunities?

> Those who need employment to live should come over and spend at least a month looking around, checking on cost of living, climate, way of life, opportunities, and wage rages.—Frank Jeckell, who moved from Canada to Hawaii in 1963 to establish the famous Wax Museum in Waikiki.

I am going to open this business-like chapter by quoting from the Chamber of Commerce pamphlet, "Living and Working In Hawaii."

Mainland students or others seeking "summer jobs" are cautioned that most seasonal jobs are filled by local residents.

Oahu is classified as a tight labor market area. This situation exists because of the lack of diversified industries and the relative immobility of the work force. Therefore, employment service officials advise that the chances of getting a job in Honolulu in most occupations are slim, and by mail they are next to impossible.

Although there is no residential requirement for federal and state jobs, civil service employment is normally confined to those already established in the islands.

For anyone coming to the islands in search of employment, the Chamber of Commerce of Hawaii cautions that they should have sufficient funds for return transportation in the event they are unsuccessful in locating suitable work.

Information is obtainable from the following agencies, all located in Honolulu.

General Employment: Hawaii State Employment Service
                       P.O. Box 3680
                       Honolulu, Hawaii 96811

Teaching: Department of Education
                       State of Hawaii
                       P.O. Box 2360
                       Honolulu, Hawaii 96804

Youth under 18:	Child Labor Office
	824 Punchbowl Street
	Honolulu, Hawaii 96813
Federal Employment:	U.S. Civil Service
	Federal Building
	Honolulu, Hawaii 96813

LICENSE REQUIREMENTS

State licenses are required to practice various trades and professions. Prerequisites in some cases include stipulated experience, examination, character references. I can include here basic information regarding only a few fields. For further information see, *Starting a Business in Hawaii,* described later in the chapter.

Architect. One to two years experience if graduate of approved curriculum—five to eleven years if not. Examination unless registered elsewhere; personal interview and short examination in any case.

Barber. Eighth-grade education or equivalent; minimum 18 months experience. Examination includes practical and written or oral tests.

Certified Public Accountant. College graduate, or equivalent. Examination. Three years of public accounting experience, two of which must have been with a CPA—five years if not.

Contractor. Four years of experience within last 10, financial statement and credit report, examination.

Hairdresser. Equivalent of high school education and 2,000 hours as a supervised apprentice, or graduation from a registered beauty school.

Dentist. Must have passed examination of the National Board of Dental Examiners and be graduate of accredited American dental school. U.S. citizen. Examination.

Engineer. Three years experience if graduate of approved curriculum—twelve years if not. Examinations required, unless registered elsewhere. In any case, personal interview and short examination.

Lawyer. For details write to Clerk, Supreme Court, Judiciary Building, Honolulu, Hawaii 96813.

Nurse. Graduates of accredited nursing schools are eligible to take the Hawaii Board examination for registered nurse licensure if the transcript shows they have met the Board's minimum curriculum requirements. Licenses are issued without examination if licenses by examination are already held in other jurisdictions of the United States.

Pharmacist. One-year experience in Hawaii or two years in another state. Examination. Graduate of approved school unless registered in another state.

Physician. Only applicants who meet all requirements and have passed FLEX with a 75 percent average or National Board examinations require no further examination.

Real Estate Salesman. Written examination.

Veterinarian. One-year residency. Graduate of accredited veterinary college.

Other trades and professions that require licenses include: abstract maker, chiropractor, cemetery salesman, collector, detective (or guard), engineer, land surveyor, masseur, optician, optometrist, osteopath, and psychologist.

WAGES

A survey of pay rates by the Hawaii Employers Council revealed the following monthly full wage range and median wage for all industry. (No doubt, wages will be higher when you read this book.)

	Full Range	*Median*
Senior Typist	$ 355 – 776	$ 467
Clerk Stenographer	325 – 915	500
Secretary	277 – 935	590
Staff Nurse	575 – 1,057	715
Medical Lab Technician	539 – 1,014	767
Licensed Civil Engineer	1,050 – 2,000	1,457
Laborer, Heavy	$1.95 – $4.50 per hr.	$2.87 per hr.

Industry in Hawaii has long been heavily unionized. (Unions are a major political force.)

THE JOB MARKET

"How can I find a job in Hawaii?" you may ask.

Unless you are fortunate enough to know someone in Hawaii

who will help you, probably the best advice is not to waste stamps and stationery in writing letters. If you can't afford a prospecting trip to Hawaii without burning your employment and other bridges behind you, many of my pollees and I suggest you wait until you can.

If you do make a prospecting trip, the agencies mentioned above are good starting points. You might profitably supplement them by checking the employment classified ads in the newspapers (at least for a temporary job).

If you are a present or former federal employee eligible for transfer or reinstatement, the U.S. Civil Service Commission will give you a list of federal establishments and their addresses so you can get in touch with them personally.

If you're a stenographer, or even a good typist, you may be in demand. I'll tell you what my wife did not too long ago. She needed temporary work in each of several quarters in order to acquire eligibility for subsequent Social Security benefits. She registered with Kelly Girl, an employment agency for temporary jobs only. Within minutes on one occasion, and overnight on another, she found pleasant temporary employment. One of the jobs was with the state government. She probably could have found a satisfactory permanent job if she had wished one. For readers who are no longer young, let me add that neither is my wife. I would not be so unchivalrous as to disclose her age at the time she obtained those jobs, but I'll give you a clue. At that time I was 61 and she is 6 years younger than I.

The labor force is distinctive for the above-average number of young persons and women. It seems clear from my many conversations with islanders that the high cost of living is responsible for the unusually large number of women workers.

The unemployment rate in Hawaii in recent years has consistently remained lower than the national average. Seasonal variation is also less than in other states. Nevertheless, as in all other states, unemployment is a costly problem in Hawaii.

The government and people of the state naturally don't want Mainlanders to add to the already burdensome welfare rolls because they can't find employment. Downright repugnant to them are people (usually young) who hie themselves to Hawaii with no intention of working, at least not steadily. Some make themselves unemployable by weird personal appearance and attire. Having done so, they line up for food coupons and welfare checks. They give a bad name to youngsters who come to seek an honest living in these easy-going, tropical islands. The deliberately unemployed, underfinanced minority group, like their counterparts elsewhere, deliberately flaunt the laws and mores of the islands, and when they are challenged by law enforcement officers and public indignation, scream and kick that they are being discriminated against. That's my sermon for today—and I hope it won't be misinterpreted by the many fine young people whom I have met in Hawaii who are studying, working, and enjoying life in these hospitable isles without abusing the hospitality of the islanders.

I should point out that most fields of employment do not offer wages commensurate with the cost of living. I've compared classified ads in San Francisco with those in Honolulu, where the cost of living is higher. No question about it, the wages offered in San Francisco are higher. This is borne out by reports of Hawaii's Labor Department, which indicate a shortage of applicants for certain positions due to low salaries offered.

Shortages in other fields exist because of unfavorable working conditions, such as irregular working hours or days, uncertain duration of jobs, location of work.

Many young people from the Mainland find employment in hotels and restaurants, particularly during the summer. For those who may seek such employment, may I add that a union spokesman described the Neighbor Island hotel labor contract as "the best in the industry anywhere." Under that agreement, wage rates are the same as in the Waikiki hotels, and fringe benefits are outstanding.

Strong persons who are willing to work hard under unfavorable conditions normally can find jobs in the pineapple fields or canneries during the summer months.

BUSINESS OPPORTUNITIES

Are you considering being boss of your own business in Hawaii? If so, I can tell you that the economic climate is healthy. Here are a few indicators.

The population is increasing steadily.

So is the per capita income. Income and consumption vary little among the ethnic groups.

Hawaii, the "Crossroads of the Pacific," is the hub of a growing Pacific commerce.

Exports are increasing steadily.

Tourism regularly sets new growth records.

The Chamber of Commerce has this to say about business opportunities:

> It is not practical for the Chamber to offer advice concerning investment possibilities and opportunities for establishing or operating specific types of enterprises in Hawaii, but its Information Office can offer help in finding source material.
>
> It is recommended that anyone interested in establishing a business in Hawaii first personally investigate local conditions before making a final decision or entering into definite financial obligations.
>
> A statistical publication, "Hawaii Facts and Figures," with detailed, current information on many facets of the State's economy is available from the Chamber of Commerce of Hawaii for $1.00 per copy including postage.

The state government assists in the establishment of new businesses and in the expansion of going concerns through loans administered by its Department of Planning and Economic Development, which offers numerous other services and issues a variety of publications, including a book entitled *Starting a Business in Hawaii,* which contains the broad state requirements applicable to all businesses and references to individual county requirements. The mailing address of this Department is P.O. Box 2359, Honolulu, Hawaii 96804. Its offices are in the Kamamalu Building, 250 South King Street.

One common problem of newcomers who wish to start a retail business is the scarcity of suitable locations. Shopping centers don't proliferate here as they do on the Mainland, and demand is heavy for existing commercial real estate. Harvey Hartenstein, of Granada Hills, California, for example, spent more than a year seeking a site for a franchised electronics business, before ending up in a theatre that was closing down because of inadequate parking space.

Speaking of franchises, there are fine opportunities in Hawaii for franchised businesses. But here as elsewhere, extreme care should be taken in buying a franchise to avoid being fleeced.

In addition to licensing and business registration, there are state (and usually county) requirements applicable to all businesses concerned with food, lodging, instruction, poisonous and hazardous materials, burial, personnel, and transportation.

I'm going to close this chapter with some sage observations of my pollees about jobs and job-seeking.

"As with Alaska, a job is most definitely needed before arriving."

"It is not the place to come without a job in hand."

"Do not move to the islands, especially with a family to support, expecting to find a job *after* you get here. Get the job first."

"Employment and good pay are hard to come by, particularly if you don't have a profession, or if you have to wait to qualify through a State examination."

"If you do not have a job awaiting you and need money to support yourself, think twice before moving here" (a teacher.)

10

What About Young People and Schools?

Living here teaches children about all kinds of people—for better understanding.—Gwen Palmer, who came here at the age of 19 and married a long-time resident.

Schools here are about average I'd say. Generally speaking, more discipline is needed (as everywhere).—Former Texan with sons in Oahu schools.

Is Hawaii a good place for young people? My pollees think so. Here are two questions I asked: (1) "Do you think Hawaii is a good place for teen-agers?" and (2) "Do you think it is a good place for pre-teen-agers?"

Seventy-one percent of the respondents think Hawaii is a good place for teen-agers. Of the negative replies, many stemmed from a distaste for irresponsible young transients, particularly on the Neighbor Islands.

A whopping 92 percent of the respondents think Hawaii is a good place for pre-teen-agers.

I found far less unanimity in reply to my question, "What do you think of the schools, public and private?" For that reason and because of the importance of the subject to parents and students, I'm going to give you a generous number of comments from each of the major islands.

OAHU (WHERE 4/5 OF HAWAII'S STUDENTS ATTEND SCHOOL)

"Private schools are almost a necessity after the 6th grade."

"Public are improving. Private are for people who feel socially inferior." (She has two children in public schools.)

"Good, but plagued with problems."

"Public are good and are trying to get better. Private are unnecessary expense" (son in public school).

"Schools do not teach enough history of the Mainland U.S.A. or geography."

"Grade schools are good."

"Private schools are too expensive. Some public schools are below average academically" (two sons in school).

"Public schools are not a good place for teen-agers."

"Most are excellent and give a wide education in racial equality."

"Private are very good; public mixed, but comparable to Mainland" (former staff member, University of Michigan).

"Public—poorest I've seen. The number and affluence of private schools attest to the generally poor opinion held" (military officer with three children, last based in California).

"A few public schools are adequate; most are poor. Private are good."

"Some public schools good, some bad. Private schools generally good—except in speech."

"Public below California standard" (two children in school).

"Public school system leaves much to be desired—too lax" (two sons in school).

"Our daughter goes to private school as we do not like the type of children who go to the public school in our area."

"Son graduated from private school. Believe it superior to public."

"Excellent. Produce enthusiastic students."

"Punahou, largest prep school in the U.S., is excellent. My son teaches there."

"Private are expensive; need improved public."

"Not quite on par with better Mainland schools" (ex-Californian).

"Private schools excellent but in financial distress. Public schools good" (former New Yorker).

HAWAII

"Limited in opportunity by ethnic imbalance (too many Japanese teachers)."

"Not very good but there are a few exceptions, both public and private."

"Compared with Mainland schools, as good as most" (three children).

"I think the school system being on a State level is far superior to Mainland school district system" (two children in school).

"Public inadequate and not improving. Private relatively expensive."

"Judging from the product, I think some abandoned practices might turn out better men and women."

"They are not as good as they should and could be."

"Public are bad. Private not too bad but snob appeal there."

"Some are good, some are very good, and some below average because of the poor English spoken by teachers and pupils."

"Better than most Mainland schools but there are problems" (a former teacher from California).

"For a *haole* public schools are tough—private o.k." (This came from Hilo.)

"Would be better if less prejudice were heard at home" (Kailua-Kona area).

"Private good, public poor" (son in school).

"Very poor from 7th to 12th grade. Elementary is good" (son 16).

KAUAI

"The teaching staff leaves a lot to be desired."

"Public schools are quite good. It's the level of many of the kids that tends to be low because of lack of home education" (clergyman).

"I think they are comparable to the Mainland" (former Los Angeleno).

"State educational system is comparable to most Mainland communities" (executive from Evanston).

"Only fair on this island. *Haole* pre-teenagers may have some trouble in school, as a minority group."

"Very modern and up to date. Better than on Mainland" (former New Yorker).

"Small amount of race prejudice."

"Public schools are making great strides in formerly neglected areas."

"I am very happy with the public grammer [sic] school—not so much with high" (four children in school).

"Public are below standard, private too exclusive."

"Our children have had some trouble at school because of being *haole*."

"*Haole* pre-teenagers may have trouble in school as a minority, but not too bad." (His son told me that he had trouble his first year, but no worse than his first year in a new school in Chicago.)

MAUI

"I find them to be somewhat behind the Mainland school where I taught but there is a definite attempt to upgrade them" (from Illinois).

"Satisfactory" (teacher).

"Excellent. I worked in the public school system for 40 years."

"Very good. Parochial schools seem quite expensive."

"Hawaii Preparatory Academy and Seabury Hall are fine private schools."

"Public schools are quite good. I don't believe in private schools anywhere, but the ones here are excellent" (two children in school).

"Schools are a little behind (but I am not in favor of public schools anyhow)" (former Ohioan).

"Public schools have tremendous variations—generally not as good as our Mainland experience" (formerly of Marin County, California. Two children in school).

"Some are below average because of poor English spoken by teachers and pupils, but some are very good" (two children).

"My children have run into a little pressure from groups at school, but it was a learning experience."

"I'm very unhappy with public schools and am now sending my son to a private one."

"All very good. Private schools are expensive" (teacher).

"I feel my granddaughters are getting a good education and also learning of other ethnic groups."

"All are fine if children come from a stable home" (retired teacher).

"They're struggling hard to keep up with today's world" (teacher).

"Excellent. Particularly the musical education."

After perusing those comments and many more, talking with students, teachers, and parents, and reading a variety of reports, I concluded that private schools are mostly excellent; that public schools vary in quality from excellent to poor; and that there is some racial intolerance in the schools. Sounds like the Mainland, doesn't it?

The hundred or so private schools are attended by almost one of every six students, which indicates their importance in Hawaiian education. Punahou, founded by the missionaries, is the largest prep school in the United States, and is universally acknowledged to be outstanding.

But, though it is the most prestigious, Punahou is not the most exclusive private school in Hawaii. That distinction goes to the Kamehameha Schools, to which children of most of my readers could not gain admittance. Kamehameha Schools, the sole beneficiary of Princess Bernice Pauahi, may be attended only by children with some Hawaiian blood.

As for the public schools, qualitative evaluation depends somewhat on the evaluator, according to a poll of parents and educators made by Hawaii's Department of Education.

From a list of 16 suggested tasks of public education, the educators selected intellectual goals as the three most important, in contrast to the three most favored by parents:

1. To teach loyalty to America and the American way of life.

2. To teach efficient use of the "3 R's"—the basic tools for acquiring and communicating knowledge.

3. To instill a sense of right and wrong; a moral standard of behavior.

Parents ranked lowest among the 16 tasks, "The need for students to accumulate a fund of information about many things."

That survey not only points to the need for harmonizing aims of parents and teachers, but also illustrates the efforts being made by the school system for improvement.

The system itself is different from its counterparts on the Mainland where states have township, city, or county school districts, each with taxing and policy-making power. In Hawaii the entire state is the school district. The State Board of Education, an elected body, sets policy for the entire state. The state legislature has the only taxing power.

It has been pointed out by experts that in theory the schools in Hawaii should all be equal, but that this is not so in practice. Why are some schools bad and some good? This is hard to answer, because even the experts can't agree on what is a *good* school. One researcher says that you can call a school good if it takes a student with a given ability, background, motivation, etc. and develops his achievement to a level beyond what might have been expected. Another admits that the overburdened public schools cannot overcome serious learning disadvantages arising from environment, such as a home where good English is not spoken.

Though there was some disagreement on the goals and quality of Hawaii's public schools, everyone seemed to applaud the addition to the curricula of a course in consumer education, the first of its type to be required for graduation from any public high school in the U.S. In the words of Jane Smith, an educational specialist who was instrumental in developing the course, "The young people know all about flower power but nothing about signature power. We've taught them how to get a job but not how to hold onto the money they're earning. The office of consumer protection receives 16,000 complaints a year from consumers. By having a course like this, we hope to prevent some of the costly heartbreaks."

As to racial intolerance in the schools, one of my pollees, who prefers to remain anonymous, has expressed what I think is the majority sentiment of parents who have moved here from the Mainland.

"The newly arrived *haole* adolescent from the Mainland suffers a not so subtle prejudice, but perhaps they will mature into stronger adults as a result of their experiences. There is much to offset this sort of thing. But if we are truly the 50th State, it is to be hoped that it will not take too many years to 'civilize' some over-rough school situations.''

May I summarize by saying that Hawaii is trying to provide schools that are good by almost any definition. The state spends more for public education than for any other purpose. And most people I talk with seem to think that the taxpayers are getting a fair return on their dollar.

Inquiries about Hawaii public and private schools should be directed to the Department of Education, P.O. Box 2360, Honolulu, Hawaii 96804.

Many young people come to Hawaii from the Mainland as students at the University or a college and decide to stay or to return here as residents, so I'm going to say a few words about Hawaii's sunny seats of higher learning.

Five privately operated colleges offer four-year programs. All are small, all are coeducational, all are on Oahu except one.

Chaminade College. Operated by the Catholic Society of Mary. Has a $7 million campus improvement program. Honolulu.

Brigham Young University, Hawaii Campus. Operated by the Church of Jesus Christ of Latter-Day Saints (Mormon) on the windward side of Oahu. Almost half of the students are foreign —from some two dozen or more countries.

Hawaii Loa College. Operated by a group of Protestant churches. Honolulu.

Hawaii Pacific College. Non-sectarian. In downtown Honolulu. Combines study with work experiences.

Mauna Olu Campus, U.S. International University. On Maui. Rustic environment.

By far the greatest number of college students in Hawaii are on the Manoa (Honolulu) campus of the University of Hawaii. The University also has a four-year campus at Hilo (Hilo College) and operates seven two-year community colleges, four of them on Oahu and one each on Kauai, Hawaii, and Maui. A medical school and a law school have recently been established.

On the Manoa campus there is a federal educational institution, the Institute for Cultural and Technical Interchange between East and West (called, for short, the East-West Center).

The Center was established in 1960 by Congress to promote better relations and understanding between the United States and the nations of Asia and the Pacific through cooperative study, training, and research. It provides specialized and advanced academic programs, as well as technological training. For every two students who come from Asia or the Pacific area, one American is selected for advanced study or research on federal grants.

A feature of the University of Hawaii long of interest to Mainland girls is the Summer Session. Many of them, and fewer Mainland boys, attend annually. Some come just for fun and sun. Some are serious students. Some are able to mix study and fun into a profitable and pleasant experience in a unique setting. And some never go home—Hawaii becomes their home.

To find out what my pollees think of the idea of Mainlanders mixing surf and summer school, I asked them, "Would you recommend summer school attendance at a Hawaiian university for a non-resident?" "Why?" Here are some representative answers.

"No. They see too easy a life too young."

"Yes. Delightful experience."

"Yes, for change of pace."

"Yes. Become acquainted with our Aloha spirit and mixed cultures" (from a man 70 years old).

"Yes. More intellectual freedom" (from a journalist).

"Would be a good experience but very costly."

"Student wouldn't study because of surroundings."

"Yes. Very educational, both culturally and in experience."

"Yes. Learn of other races and cultures."

"Yes. If they come to study and not to demonstrate" (former Colorado teacher).

"Yes. They would come back later to live here."

"Yes. Good staff."

"No. The university is rabid with rabble rousers, including profs."

"Yes. To learn something of Pacific-Asian-Hawaiian cultures."

"No. I don't think they accomplish much."

"No. Overcrowded already."

"Yes. Broaden geographic and ethnic experiences."

"No. Too promiscuous during summer" (from Beverly Hills).

"No. Just a lark."

"What better place to spend a summer?"

"Yes. Variety in recreation and living conditions."

"No. Too much permissiveness."

"Yes. Not for credit, just for fun."

"Yes. Hawaii is more than beaching and drinking."

"If stable youngster, a nice experience."

"Yes. New people and customs but still America."

"Even just a summer in Hawaii is better than nothing."

"Living with mixed races is a good experience for Mainlanders."

"For serious study I would choose a more conservative school."

"From my observation it looks like Berkeley."

"No. *Haoles* just won't adjust. They want to change us."

Summer school courses range from belly dancing to advanced calculus. Somewhere in between is one my wife wants to take: the intermediate course in Chinese cooking.

Adults can choose from a wide variety of evening courses (not necessarily for credit) at the University and at high schools all over Hawaii. Courses of study range from abacus to yoga, and include such locally oriented offerings as bonsai, calligraphy, guitar, hula, Japanese flower arranging, orchid culture, Polynesian craft and dances, shellcraft jewelry, and ukelele. The course titles that have intrigued me most are *What Every Parent Should Know About Drugs* and *Football Fundamentals for Women*. Drug abuse and football are taken seriously in Hawaii.

11

Is Hawaii a Good Place for Retirement?

> Not a place to retire unless you have several hobbies to keep you occupied. Also unless you have a substantial income, you are in trouble.—Paul V. Wendell, formerly of Millbrae, California.

Probably the most important decision relating to retirement for the average person is where to live. Should one leave his present location? On this let me quote from a pamphlet of the Social Security Administration:

The vast majority of people want to stay in their present communities when they retire. They value the memories that go with their homes. They want to keep them as a place for the children to come back to. They want to be near old friends, neighbors, and younger members of the family. They want to go on in their churches, clubs, and fraternal societies with people they know.

According to one survey in a Northern State, almost 80 out of every 100 elect to stay in their home State. And a good decision it is, too, for the kind of people discussed above, particularly if they own their own homes.

The pamphlet goes on to say:

Moving to another part of the country should be planned with great care. People have sold their homes and moved to a new location without finding out much about it, only to discover too late that it wasn't what they had expected.

The best way to find out about living costs, the chances for making new friends, and getting part-time work in other places is by taking a vacation in the other location or visiting there for awhile after retirement. This way the old home is there to go back to if things don't work out.

Even before visiting, some things can be found out about the new community—such things as the kind of climate throughout the year as well as kinds of transportation, businesses, recreation, and churches. Such information may be had from the public library or by writing to the Chamber of Commerce in the new community.

Now then, with that caution against a rash decision to move to Hawaii behind me, I'd like to discuss salient aspects of living here as a retiree.

ACTIVITIES FOR RETIREES

The indolent, tropical scene can breed languor and a drinking problem for retirees who lack avocational interests. Sherman Cannon, who retired to Hawaii a decade ago, states the case well.

"Do not fail to take active interest in *something*—preferably many things. Vegetating on retirement is merely waiting for demise. And if you desire happiness, concern yourself with constructive activities (not mere amusements), living to help others."

I know of no place that provides more opportunity than Hawaii for those activities so vital to happy retirement. If a catalyst is needed, dozens of centers and clubs for seniors are eager to help. Where else would you find seniors studying hula dancing and ukelele strumming?

Now that I've carefully used the word "seniors" twice, I'd like your permission to switch to "senior citizen." I am aware that some object to that term as a euphemism associated with the world of politics and advertising. Nevertheless, it is so widely used in Hawaii that it would be awkward to disavow it in this book.

SENIOR CITIZEN ORGANIZATIONS

Retirees moving to Hawaii from the Mainland would find themselves at home at the Makua Alii Senior Center, 1541 Kalakaua Avenue, Honolulu. This center, on the ground floor of an apartment for senior citizens, stresses hobbies, clubs, and social activities. It is here that the Honolulu chapter of the American Association of Retired Persons meets each Wednesday at 1 P.M. for a program followed by coffee and cookies.

There are numerous senior citizen clubs, some with ethnic or religious affiliations, throughout Hawaii.

The Honolulu Office of Social Resources publishes a *Senior Citizen Handbook* that is a boon to the elderly. It lists emergency telephone numbers, nursing homes, retirement homes, and senior citizen clubs and organizations. Also listed are the proper contacts on such matters as adult education, consumer protection, legal assistance, employment, insurance, personal counseling, and housing. In addition, there are sections covering shopping hints, how to buy a used car, how not to be cheated in business transactions, how to find the true interest rate, and discounts for the elderly. The handbook can be obtained from the Information and Referral Services of the Honolulu Committee on Aging, 623 South Beretania Street, Honolulu, Hawaii 96813.

DISCOUNTS AND PRIVILEGES

The list of discounts and other privileges for the elderly in Hawaii grows constantly. Some of those I have listed below are applicable on Oahu only.

1. Passengers 65 or older ride free on Honolulu's city-owned bus line.

2. Residents 60 years or older who are fully retired can play golf on Oahu's several municipal courses for $12 a year, the cost of an annual pass. That's the biggest golfing bargain I know of except at the famed St. Andrews course in Scotland, where the local villagers can play the fabulous course for an annual fee of about $3.50. Oh yes, anyone can play free on the 9-hole course of the Dole Pineapple Company on Lanai.

3. Residents 65 or over may buy a $5 membership card from either of the major inter-island airlines and be entitled to flights on a space-available basis at a substantial discount.

4. At least one theatre chain offers discounts to senior citizens during off-peak hours on certain days.

5. Some drugstores allow discounts on prescription drugs.

6. Some firms allow discounts on eyeglass purchases.

7. Special tax exemptions.

COST OF LIVING

You know by now that I wouldn't kid you about the cost of living in Hawaii. It is high, even for retirees. I fully agree with numerous pollees whose message could be paraphrased, "It's no fun in the sun without 'mon.' "

How much "mon" depends somewhat on the individual or couple. Some manage to live modestly and to effect economies in amazing ways. One of the best money-saving methods I know of for retirees is to swap baby-sitting services for such things as grass-cutting, window-washing, floor-polishing, etc. This arrangement also enables the older generation to keep acquainted with the younger ones.

The financial aspect of decision-making is one of the reasons I advise retirees and near-retirees, as well as anyone else contemplating a free-choice move to Hawaii, not to burn their bridges. Make a careful exploratory trip first, and if you can't afford it, don't move.

HOUSING

Even with all the money in the world, retirees who move to Hawaii or elsewhere have to consider many factors in choosing their housing. Some will be happiest in an age-segregated community or retirement home, others in a neighborhood with people of various ages. Other important considerations: adequate lighting; freedom from irritating noises; safety aspects of floors, steps, and furnishings; availability of doctors; proximity of hospitals; adequacy of shopping facilities.

The only item mentioned in the preceding paragraph that seems to require elaboration in this chapter is retirement homes. I know of only three major ones in Hawaii, all on Oahu. All are highly regarded.

The Laniolu, 333 Lewers Street, is in the heart of Waikiki not far from the ocean. Laniolu is a Hawaiian word meaning "Haven of Rest." The non-denominational home is operated by the American Lutheran Church. It occupies a 12-story building topped by the Prince of Peace Lutheran Church.

Accommodations offered are studios for single occupancy

and bedroom units for double occupancy. All are nicely furnished and have lanais and a view of either the shoreline or the mountains. The monthly charge includes meals, weekly maid service, and incidental nursing care. Four floors are occupied by an infirmary with both intensive and intermediate care facilities. Reception, dining, and lounge areas occupy the first two floors.

Arcadia, 1434 Punahou Street, Honolulu, is owned and well operated by Central Union Church, a member of the United Church of Christ. It is open to persons of all faiths. The location, on a quiet street almost in Honolulu's geographic center, is convenient by public transportation to cultural, recreational, and shopping facilities.

The high-rise accommodations are studios and one-bedroom units, each with kitchenette and lanai. Indoor and outdoor recreational facilities abound.

A monthly charge provides for meals, non-personal laundry, maid service bi-weekly, utilities, and health care at nominal cost in the Medicare-approved Health Care Center.

Pohai Nani (meaning "surrounded by beauty") is on the windward side of Oahu at 45-090 Namoku Street, Kaneohe, not far from Kaneohe Bay. It is operated by Pacific Homes, a non-profit corporation of the United Methodist Church. The location of the 14-story main building and cottages is quiet and scenic with a mountain backdrop. The excellent recreational facilities include a heated pool. Within a mile is a golf course. Downtown Honolulu is twenty minutes away by free private bus.

Accommodations range from studios to two-bedroom cottages, mostly with kitchenettes, all with lanais or patios. The monthly service charge includes meals, semi-monthly maid service, utilities, and nursing services in an adjoining facility. For an increased monthly charge, physician's services, prescription medicines, therapy, surgery, and hospitalization can be included.

All of those homes require an entrance fee. I am not including any cost figures, because the rate structures are complicated and subject to change.

WRAP-UP

Perhaps it's an unwarranted digression, but I'm going to put in a paragraph here to suggest to retirees everywhere in the United States that they consider joining the American Association of Retired Persons. The address is 1909 K Street, Washington, D.C. 20006. The cost is only $2 a year. For that you get benefits too numerous to list here. Local chapters, including some I've visited in Hawaii, provide fellowship and stimulating, informative programs.

A subscription to the magazine *Retirement Living* is another good way to keep up with what's going on among and for senior citizens. The cost is $6 a year. The address is 99 Garden Street, Marion, Ohio 43302.

And to anyone thinking of retiring to Hawaii (or anywhere else), I highly recommend reading *How to Avoid the Retirement Trap* by Leland and Lee Cooley (Nash Publishing).

Now back to Hawaii. Hawaii is worth a good look for retirees who have sufficient money to live here comfortably, *provided* they (1) have or could develop avocations to keep them busy, (2) enjoy tropical living, and (3) do not have such close ties to the Mainland that they would regret the distance that separates them.

On the important matter of health, consider this: A study of 3,000 prominent men and women of Hawaii with a median age of 56 revealed a death rate of 11 per thousand per year, compared with 16.5 for the national norm of such an age group.

12

Do You Have to Learn the Hawaiian Language?

Hawaiian, as far as the language goes, is easy, but until a newly arrived Mainlander learns some of the basic words he can be embarrassed.—Buck Buchanan, radio announcer from Hollywood.

To me it's a wonder that when they were deciding on a nickname for Hawaii, they didn't choose "The Tri-language State." English is, of course, *the* language of Hawaii. But the state has two languages all its own: Hawaiian and Pidgin. Anyone living in Hawaii, or even visiting, comes in contact with both, so a little knowledge of them at the outset is useful.

Except on the island of Niihau, where it is still the mother tongue, the Hawaiian language is spoken in a dwindling number of homes, but it is not a dying language. It is widely heard in songs and in isolated words and phrases.

The basic rules of pronunciation are said to be simple, but I have observed that authorities don't always agree. The rules that follow I have distilled from various sources. They should give you a reasonable facsimile of correct pronunciation (says he, perhaps the world's worst language student).

1. Pronounce the consonants (h, k, l, m, n, p, w) as in English, except that if "w" is the next to the last letter in a word pronounce it like a "v." For example, Ewa is pronounced as if spelled with a "v."

2. Pronounce the vowels as in Spanish or Latin, i.e., "a" as in father, "e" as in they, "i" as in machine, "o" as in no, and "u" as in dude.

3. A syllable consists of one vowel, which may be preceded by a consonant as in hu-la. Remember that each consonant

starts a new syllable and that all syllables end with a single vowel (a second one would be a new syllable, as in hu-i).

4. Pronounce each syllable separately, except for eight pairs (ae, ai, ao, au, ei, eu, oi, ou) which are supposed to be merged into one sound with emphasis on the sound of the first vowel (which I find difficult).

5. Stress is generally on the next to the last syllable. Exceptions: The first syllable of a five-syllable word gets equivalent stress; those eight vowel pairs get the stress whenever they appear; any vowel with a macron (horizontal line) over it gets the stress.

6. A glottal stop (looks like a reversed apostrophe) calls (theoretically, at least) for a brief pause, as if your breath gave out. Some words start with a glottal stop. How you're supposed to pause for that I don't know.

An important thing to remember about the pronunciation is not to get in a hurry. Take as a classic example, *humuhumunukunukuapua'a,* the name of the fish mentioned in the song *Little Grass Shack.* It may look hopeless at first. But try pronouncing it slowly, one syllable at a time. It comes out something like this: *hu-mu-hu-mu-nu-ku-nu-ku-AH-pu-a-*(pause)*a.* Now you no longer need slur over it when you sing *Little Grass Shack.*

If you'd like to practice your pronunciation, you may do so on the following list of commonly used words (which appear without macrons or glottal stops, as is usually the case in printed matter).

ae—yes
ahi—fire
aikane—friend
aole—no
auwe—alas
hale—house
hana—work
hapa haole—half-Caucasian
hapai—pregnant
heiau—ancient temple

lolo—dumb
mahalo—thanks
makai—toward the sea
mauka—toward the mountains
mele—song
menehuene—legendary pixie
nani—pretty
ono—delicious
paakiki—stubborn

honi—kiss	*pali*—cliff
huhu—angry	*paniolo*—cowboy
hui—club	*pau*—finished
ipo—sweetheart	*pilikia*—trouble
kai—ocean	*poho*—out of luck
kala—money	*pua*—flower
kane—man	*punee*—couch
kapu—taboo	*pupu*—hors d'oeuvre
kaukau—food (pidgin)	*pupule*—crazy
keiki—child	*wahini*—woman
kokua—help	*wikiwiki*—hurry

The pronunciation of most of those words is not difficult but pronouncing some place-names is. Almost all place-names in the state are in the Hawaiian language, so it would behoove you, should you wish to ask directions to the Kalanianaole highway or even the short street in Honolulu named Oo, to learn the basic rules of pronunciation.

Now let's take a brief look at Pidgin as spoken in Hawaii.

Some say that it is as distinct a language as French, Spanish, or Russian. Others dub it a dialect. In any case, it is the language most commonly spoken—sometimes the only language spoken—in many homes in Hawaii. Some youths and their elders use it as an "in" language or when they do not wish to offend associates who do not speak standard English.

Pidgin has been described as shorthand English because it omits unnecessary words, runs words together, drops syllables, and endings. The order of words, too, is not the same as in English.

The classic example is *da kine,* derived from "the kind" or "that kind." When accompanied by appropriate gestures and facial expressions, it can mean almost anything according to context. It can be used as a crutch by a speaker who doesn't know just what he wants to say. It has been compared to *you know, thingamajig, thataway.*

Examples of dropped letters and syllables can be found in expressions like *shave ice* and *toss salad.*

As to the order of words and an indication of why pidgin exists, there is the story of the immigrant mother who corrects her son for asking "Where you was?" She explains (incorrectly) that he should have said, "Where was you?"

Some old-timers advise that newcomers treat pidgin as jargon, not to be taken seriously except by persons who wish to learn it.

Here are some comments of pollees:

"I like to listen to Pidgin English when I don't have a technical discussion going. I think it is a fun language and that those who use it well understand this and have fun with it. It sure makes it less than fun when one is trying to get a difficult point across on some technical subject, however, and the other party doesn't speak anything but pidgin" (a military officer).

"I enjoy trying to understand the pidgin of some of the immigrants—particularly gardeners who can understand English in the main but still do what they want despite my attempts to speak their pidgin" (after eight years on Oahu).

Another pollee advises, "Don't try it—it will mark you as a newcomer."

Pidgin is not something to joke about in the schools of Hawaii. Many children speak only pidgin when they enter school, which makes the task of both pupil and teacher difficult, particularly since many teachers are not masters of pidgin.

In Hilo the problem was attacked by a group of high school students, who wrote a textbook *Introduction to Hawaiian Pidgin* for newcomers, including teachers. They advise newcomers not to try to speak it. At the same time, the authors advise students to "No speak pejen en fron otha peeple."

Which reminds me of a story told by a lady on Oahu:

"After wearing false eyelashes almost all day I took them off when the wind started to blow, and having no more suitable place, dropped them into my coin purse. Later I stopped at a small Japanese grocery store and pulled out some quarters to pay for my purchase. Both eyelashes had stuck to one quarter. With a perfectly straight face, *papasan* said, 'First time I see money who see where it going.' "

And for a wrap-up, here's a story from Mrs. von Stroheim of Kauai, which speaks eloquently for itself, not only of the Pidgin but of the people of Hawaii.

"A local boy home from college was struggling valiantly to make a coconut hat for my daughter. A tourist came up to him and wanted him to make one for her sister. He replied in absolutely unintelligible sort-of Pidgin. She kept trying to communicate and he kept coming back with a jumbled mess. Finally she gave up and walked away. I reproached him for not speaking the beautiful English he was capable of, and he said, 'You know if I told her that I was about to lose my mind finishing the hat I'm doing, she would think I was trying to get out of doing one for her sister and then she'd be hurt. The fact that she couldn't understand me at all will give her something to talk about and the whole incident will become a memory of that quaint native boy on the beach.' "

13

What Do They Eat There That's Different?

I eat with chopsticks when appropriate. I eat everything—and enjoy it—so I am accepted (and cause amazement and amusement for the local people) almost everywhere I go.—Marianne Bullock, Maui librarian from San Diego.

Rare is the ex-Mainlander who eats in Hawaii as on the Mainland. I'm one of the rare ones, simply because my wife cooks international-style wherever we are—and does a good job of it, if I may say so.

Melva has long been acquainted on a cook-it-yourself basis with the dishes of China, Japan, the Philippines, Korea, and Portugal—to name the foreign cuisines most commonly served in the homes and restaurants of Hawaii in addition to Hawaiian (Polynesian) and *haole* foods.

She collaborated a few years ago with Ray Coté, owner-manager of Villa Montaña, an outstanding inn in Morelia, Mexico, in the preparation of an unusual cookbook called *Villa Montaña Cuisine*, which has sold by the thousands at the Villa. I mention those things to justify the inclusion in this chapter of a small selection of her recipes (with my comments) as representative of the cuisines you may enjoy in Hawaii.

Many ex-Mainlanders agree with me that one of the big plusses of living in Hawaii is the opportunity to partake frequently of the varied cuisines of Hawaii. The aim of this chapter is to point your way to the enjoyment of those cuisines, wherever you may be.

HAWAIIAN

I'm sure you know that a *luau* is a Hawaiian feast, usually served outdoors. Let me give you a basic menu.

Kalua pig (roasted in a pit called an *imu*)
Poi (paste made from taro root)
Lomi salmon (salted salmon mixed with
  tomatoes and onions)
Chicken luau (with taro leaves and coconut
  milk)
Sweet potatoes (baked in the pit)
Pineapple spears
Bananas (baked in the pit)
Coconut pudding (*haupia*)

I'm not going to give you the recipes for any of those delicacies; they're dealt with in many cookbooks. Nor will I give you such exotics as *Princess Papooli's Pickled Papaya*. I think it would be more useful to give you a few of Melva's Hawaiian-style specialties.

Chicken Coconut Casserole

I've seen a somewhat similar dish prepared with tuna. I prefer Melva's version made with breast of chicken. As to the half coconuts that this is baked in: save them and eat the coconut meat later as snacks. This recipe and all that follow make 6 servings unless otherwise indicated.

3 coconuts
3 whole chicken breasts, boned, skinned, and
  cubed
3 tablespoons butter
2 tablespoons sesame oil
6 tablespoons flour
3 cups milk
1½ teaspoons powdered chicken soup base
  Pepper, cracked or freshly ground, to taste
2 tablespoons fresh parsley, finely minced
1 finger of ginger, chopped, or 2 teaspoons
  crystallized ginger, chopped
¼ teaspoon Five Spice Powder (very powerful
  —use with caution)
1 can pimientos, small, cut in strips
1 cup canned pineapple, diced

1. Strip fiber from coconuts. Saw in half crosswise so each half can sit upright in a shallow baking pan.

2. Saute chicken over medium heat in butter. Remove from skillet.

3. Add sesame oil to the skillet and make a white sauce with the flour and milk.

4. Add the chicken soup base, pepper, parsley, ginger, Five Spice Powder, pimientos, pineapple, and chicken.

5. Add salt only if necessary to your taste.

6. Fill coconut halves with chicken mixture.

7. Bake 1 hour at 350°.

Five Spice Powder can be purchased in any Chinese store, often elsewhere, or you can make your own. One formula calls for equal quantities of anise, cinnamon, star anise, cinnamon, cloves, and fennel; another for equal quantities of cassia, anise, fennel, cloves and ginger.

Hawaiian Beef Patties

I'm fond of tasty meat patties, particularly the ones that Melva makes on the grill, in the oven, and—when we're in the mountains—in the fireplace.

        2 pounds lean beef, ground
     ½ cup onion, minced
        2 tablespoons fresh ginger, chopped very fine
        1 tablespoon chives, chopped
        1 teaspoon parsley, chopped
        1 large clove garlic, chopped
     1½ teaspoons salt or seasoning salt
     ½ teaspoon pepper, cracked or freshly ground
     ½ cup crumbs, or cereal flakes, crushed
        1 large can of sliced pineapple, drained, or 6
           thick slices of fresh pineapple
           Honey

1. Combine all ingredients except pineapple.

2. Mix thoroughly, but lightly. Shape loosely into 6 round patties a bit larger than the pineapple slices.

3. Place patties in broiler pan.

4. Arrange pineapple slices on cookie sheet. Pour a bit of honey on top of each slice.

5. Put meat under broiler and at the same time, place pineapple in oven.

6. When meat is done to your taste, remove from broiler and place pineapple slices under broiler for a minute or so.

7. Serve pineapple slices on top of meat.

Pineapple Chutney

This is one of the "sideboys" we serve when Melva makes curry. She says that it can be converted into mango chutney by substituting green diced or sliced mangoes. Or you can make what I call manapple chutney: half mango, half pineapple.

>   3–5 small red peppers, seeded and finely
>   chopped
>   1 cup vinegar
>   ½ cup lime juice
>   1½ cups brown sugar
>   1½ cups seedless raisins
>   1 cup currants, if available (otherwise use 2½
>   cups raisins)
>   2 tablespoons finely chopped fresh ginger
>   root, or grated dried ginger root, or 3
>   tablespoons crystallized ginger, chopped
>   2 tablespoons finely chopped garlic
>   1 tablespoon salt
>   4 cups chopped pineapple
>   1 cup macadamia nuts or almonds, chopped

1. Grind chili peppers.

2. Add all ingredients except pineapple and nuts.

3. Slowly bring to a boil.

4. Add pineapple and simmer until pineapple is tender, about 30 minutes.

5. Add nuts and cook until chutney has thickened to your taste.

6. Stir frequently (scorches very easily).

7. Seal in sterilized jars. Makes approximately four pints.

Macadamia Nut Pie

Macadamia nut pie is proudly served in the best restaurants and homes of Hawaii. Usually it is a cream pie. This one is deliciously different. It is based on Melva's favorite recipe for pecan pie, which was given to her by my sister, Mrs. Roy Creasey of Mexico, Missouri.

¾ cup sugar
2 tablespoons flour, sifted
2 eggs
1 pinch salt
¼ cup milk
1 cup dark corn syrup
3 tablespoons butter, melted
1 cup macadamia nuts, sliced or chopped

1. Mix sugar and flour.
2. Beat eggs until lemon yellow in color and add to sugar and flour mixture.
3. Add milk, salt, syrup and melted butter. Mix thoroughly.
4. Cover bottom of unbaked pie crust with macadamia nuts and very carefully pour the sugar mixture on top.
5. Bake at 450° for 10 minutes, then for 20–30 minutes more at 325°.

CHINESE

I'm told that recipes for Chinese cuisine weren't invented until the twentieth century, and then only in Western countries. Many of Melva's best recipes are in her head and change with each cooking. Here are her current versions of Chinese favorites. Put them all together and you've got a memorable Chinese meal.

Shrimp with Walnuts

Melva had this dish at the Grand Hotel in Taipei for dinner. She had it again for luncheon next day. Her recipe differs from that of the Grand, but the product tastes as good.

1 cup walnuts
2 pounds fresh shrimp
½ cup Chinese rice wine or dry sherry
1 teaspoon sugar
1 clove garlic, mashed
1 teaspoon fresh ginger, very finely chopped

2 tablespoons soy sauce
3 tablespoons sesame seed oil
1 tablespoon cornstarch

1. Blanch walnuts and fry in hot oil until a golden hue. Remove nuts and drain on piece of brown paper.

2. Shell shrimp, remove sand, rinse in water, and drain.

3. Marinate shrimp for at least one hour in mixture of wine, sugar, garlic, ginger, soy sauce, and one tablespoon sesame oil.

4. Heat remaining oil in heavy skillet.

5. Put shrimp into skillet, cooking gently so the shrimp cooks but does not get tough.

6. Add cornstarch to marinade, stir until dissolved, then pour mixture in pan with shrimp, constantly stirring until sauce thickens.

7. Salt to taste.

8. Add walnuts just before serving.

Beef with Oyster Sauce and Chinese Peas

Oyster sauce is a delicious addition to many Chinese dishes. You can make it yourself, but it is a long and involved process. The thick grayish-brown liquid can be purchased in bottles in most Chinese or import grocery stores.

1½ pounds beef tenderloin, sliced paper thin
    into long strips cut against the grain
1 tablespoon cornstarch
1 teaspoon soy sauce
1 teaspoon sugar
2 tablespoons of sherry, rice wine, or vodka
3 tablespoons sesame oil (any vegetable oil
    will do)
½ teaspoon powdered pepper or freshly
    ground pepper
1 teaspoon powdered chicken base
¼ cup oyster sauce
½ cup thinly sliced onions
1 large clove garlic, minced
1 package frozen Chinese snow peas (or very
    young peas in pods), blanched

1. Marinate meat in mixture of cornstarch, soy sauce, sugar, sherry, 1 tablespoon of the sesame oil, cracked pepper, powdered chicken base, and oyster sauce at least an hour (overnight is better).

2. Heat remaining oil in skillet, add the meat mixture, and stir-fry.

3. Add onion and garlic, stir-fry for one minute.

4. Add blanched snow peas. Cook one more minute. Serve.

Lychee Chicken Salad

The lychee (also spelled *litchi, lichee,* and *laichi*) is a fruit (not a nut) that looks like a strawberry and tastes as good, fresh or canned. Of Chinese origin, it is popular in Hawaii with all races. Lychees are popular in many combinations, of which this is a savory one. An unusual luncheon dish.

    2 cups chicken breast
    ½ teaspoon ginger root, minced, or 1 teaspoon
        crystallized ginger, chopped
    ½ teaspoon powdered chicken base
    1 tablespoon lemon juice
    1 tablespoon soy sauce
    ½ teaspoon grated orange rind
      Pinch of onion salt
    ⅔ cup mayonnaise
    1 medium can lychees
    2 small cans mandarin oranges
      Lettuce, watercress, or chinese cabbage

1. Tear the chicken meat from the cooked breasts in pieces, about an inch long. This gives a better surface for absorbing the seasonings.

2. Add the ginger root, chicken base, lemon juice, soy sauce, orange rind, and onion salt to the chicken. Mix thoroughly.

3. Chill, stirring occasionally.

4. Drain oranges and lychees, reserving 1 tablespoon lychee syrup. Chill.

5. Combine mayonnaise and the tablespoon of lychee syrup. Chill.

6. Just before serving, combine all ingredients, mixing lightly.

7. Serve on crisp lettuce leaves, watercress, or chopped chinese cabbage.

Heavenly Fried Rice

A good way to use leftover meats and rice. A great accompaniment to the preceding meat dishes. Vegetables are usually cut fine and cooked quickly, just long enough to preserve the fresh color and the pleasing crunchiness. One theory is that this method of cooking developed from the lack of fuel in China. Whatever the reason, the result is food fit for the gods!

> 4 cups cooked rice, at least one day old
> 5 tablespoons sesame oil, or other vegetable oil
> 1 cup smoked ham, cooked and cut into match-stick sized strips
> ¼ cup celery, diced
> ½ cup green onions, sliced, including tops
> 1 clove garlic, minced
> 1 teaspoon ginger root, minced
> 1 tablespoon powdered chicken base
> Cracked pepper to taste
> 1 cup cooked shrimp, chopped
> 3 eggs, beaten
> ½ cup fresh parsley leaves, chopped
> 2 tablespoons soy sauce
> ½ cup almond halves, blanched, halved, and crisped in the oven

1. Loosen the grains of cooked rice with your hands.

2. Heat 2 tablespoons of the oil in a heavy skillet, toss in the ham and celery. When celery looks transparent, add remaining oil, onions, garlic, ginger, chicken base, pepper, shrimp, and rice.

3. Toss until each grain of rice is slightly coated with the oil.

4. Make a hole in center of rice mixture, pour in the beaten eggs and when they are semi-cooked, stir until blended.

5. Stir in the parsley leaves and sprinkle with soy sauce.

6. Pour into serving dish. Top with the almond halves. Serve.

For variety, you may add green bell peppers, mushrooms, bamboo shoots, water chestnuts, tender green peas, or other left-over vegetables. For even more variety you can take a tip from the Indonesians and add crisp shredded coconut, ground peanuts, and raisins (which have been made plump by soaking in a bit of hot water).

Almond Cookies

Almond cookies are as Chinese (to the Chinese) as apple pie to Americans. Here's a simple recipe that makes approximately 2 dozen cookies.

> 1½ cup flour
> ⅔ cup sugar
> 1 teaspoon salt
> ½ teaspoon baking soda
> 1 large egg
> 1 stick butter
> ½ teaspoon almond extract
> 1 egg yolk, beaten with 1 tablespoon water
> red food coloring or blanched almonds

1. Sift flour, salt, and baking soda.
2. Beat egg with fork.
3. Cream sugar and butter. Add almond extract.
4. Add egg mixture to creamed sugar, butter, almond mixture.
5. Add flour, salt and soda mixture. Sift and fold in slowly.
6. Knead thoroughly.
7. Shape into balls, the size of walnuts. Place on greased cookie tin. Make a depression in the center of each ball, with your thumb. Each cookie should be about one inch apart.
8. Brush top of each cookie with the egg-yolk and water mixture.
9. To decorate, dip the end of a chopstick in red food coloring and press into top of each cookie (the red signifies joy and good fortune) or place a blanched almond in the center.
10. Bake at 350° for about 10 minutes until light brown.

JAPANESE

To you perhaps the thought of Japanese cuisine brings to mind sukiyaki and tempura. Cookbooks bulge with recipes for those popular dishes. I'll be content to give you Melva's tonkatsu (deep-fried pork cutlets), chicken yakitori, teriyaki marinade, and her special method of preparing piping hot green tea, which goes so well with Japanese foods.

Chicken Yakitori

Almost as popular in Honolulu as in Tokyo is this chicken dish. Melva puts more ingredients in than most cooks do. Don't tell her I said so, but I think if you omitted one or two it wouldn't make much difference—but be sure to put in the chicken.

       3 whole chicken breasts, skinned and boned
       2 carrots, pared
       1 green pepper, cubed
       ½ pound fresh mushrooms, peeled
       ⅓ cup soy sauce
       3 tablespoons honey, or ¼ cup sugar
       1 teaspoon ginger root, crushed
       1 clove garlic, crushed
       1 tablespoon rice wine or sauterne

1. Cut chicken in 1-inch cubes.
2. Cut carrots crosswise into ¼-inch pieces.
3. Cook carrots and cubed green pepper for 2 minutes in a small amount of boiling water. Add mushrooms and cook for an additional 2 minutes. Remove from water.
4. Combine soy sauce, honey, ginger root, garlic, and wine for marinade.
5. Put chicken, green pepper, carrot slices, and mushrooms on bamboo or thin metal skewers. Marinate for at least 15 minutes in the soy mixture.
6. Place on rack of broiler pan and broil for 5 minutes. Turn, baste, and broil an additional 3 minutes.

Tonkatsu (Pork Cutlets)

When I've run into this in a Japanese restaurant, I've been tempted to ask how come they use cutlets rather than big juicy pork chops. I asked Melva a day or so ago, and she said maybe cutlets are less fattening. My reaction was that with all those other ingredients, this dish would be fattening if made with just a porker's squeal. Anyway, here it is for the weight-watchless.

6 pork cutlets
1 cup crumbs: half bread crumbs and half
    bran flake crumbs
½ cup flour, sifted
2 eggs, beaten
    Deep fat—enough to cover cutlets when
      frying.
3 tablespoons chili sauce or catsup
1 tablespoon honey
2 tablespoons soy sauce
    Juice of one clove of garlic
    Powdered Japanese pepper or red pepper
      sauce, to taste

1. Pound cutlets to tenderize. Sprinkle very lightly with salt.
2. Heat deep fat to 375°.
3. Dredge pork in flour, dip in eggs, and coat with the crumb mixture.
4. Fry pork in deep fat until golden brown. Drain on brown paper.
5. Combine last five ingredients. Heat and serve over pork cutlets.

Teriyaki Marinade

Excellent for marinating chicken, beef, fish, or spareribs. We frequently use it as a seasoning for vegetables. Ginger root is the key ingredient. We try to grow our own, but it can be purchased in most cities in Japanese or Chinese grocery stores.

½ cup soy sauce
3 tablespoons honey
1 tablespoon ginger root, diced very fine
3 tablespoons rice wine or sauterne
⅓ cup sesame oil or other vegetable oil
1 green onion, minced

1. Put all ingredients in a pint jar and shake well to blend.
2. Chicken and fish need to be marinaded twenty minutes or so.
3. Flank steak is one of our favorites with this marinade. Score steak, sprinkle meat tenderizer on both sides, and let it set

for 30 minutes. Cover with marinade and place in refrigerator until you are ready to broil the steak. Best if left in refrigerator 24 hours before broiling. For maximum tenderness, cut meat diagonally when serving.

Green Tea

The most important beverage of the Japanese is tea—green tea. They do not use sugar, lemon, or cream. It is served piping hot and rather weak, and in small porcelain cups without handles or saucers. Because of the large amounts of salty soy sauce used in many Japanese dishes, they consume large amounts of tea. Although green tea is the most popular, they do drink some oolong, and for very festive occasions they sometimes flavor their tea with salted cherry blossoms.

> 1 scant teaspoon green tea per cup
> Boiling water (always use *fresh* water)

1. Pour boiling water in teapot to warm it.
2. While teapot is warming, place a skillet over a medium flame, holding the pan over the flame for about 30 seconds only. Remove from flame, toss in the green tea you are going to use, shake the skillet vigorously so the tea has no opportunity to scorch. Heating the tea leaves brings out the full-bodied flavor of the tea.
3. Empty teapot, toss in the warmed tea leaves, and pour the water (just under boiling) over the tea leaves.
4. Allow to steep a moment, then swirl gently to make sure all the leaves are equally dampened.
5. Strain and pour.

Step 2 has been used for generations by the family of our friend, Consuela Kobashi, a Japanese-Mexican who has taught Melva many culinary tricks.

FILIPINO

Pork, poultry, and rice predominate in the Filipino diet. From the Spanish they got their taste for garlic, tomatoes, and onions. Sweet potatoes and bananas, too, are very popular. Here are Melva's recipes featuring these ingredients. They add up to a delicious meal.

Pork Adobo

This is the best-known Filipino dish, and to me the best tasting. Can be made from pork, chicken, fish, or beef. Or let yourself go with such combinations as chicken and pork, pork and clams, etc.

    6 lean pork chops, 1″ thick (or strips of pork,
        pencil thick, about 1 inch long)
    ¼ cup lemon juice
    2 tablespoons soy sauce
    3 tablespoons vinegar
    2 tablespoons oil
    2 cloves garlic, mashed
    ½ teaspoon cracked or freshly ground pepper
    1 tablespoon lemon peel, finely grated
    ½ teaspoon nutmeg
    ¼ teaspoon cloves
    1 teaspoon fresh ginger, minced, or ½
        teaspoon powdered ginger
    1 small stick cinnamon
    2 tablespoons paprika

1. Combine all the ingredients above and marinate in the refrigerator over night.

2. Pour the meat and marinade in a heavy iron skillet, and add water just to cover meat.

3. Cook over medium heat, stirring often, until pork is crispy and all the liquid absorbed.

4. If you prefer it with a gravy, drain off liquid as soon as meat is tender.

5. Add one tablespoon of oil to meat in pan and saute pork until brown and crispy.

6. Add sufficient flour to drained-off liquid to make a gravy.

7. Serve gravy as a side dish.

Sweet Potato Patties

Of all the root crops, sweet potatoes rank first in popularity. They are eaten raw, boiled, baked, fried. Of the many ways that Melva prepares sweet potatoes, this is my favorite.

    2 cups raw grated sweet potatoes
    3 tablespoons butter, browned

    1 tablespoon sesame seed oil
    ¼ cup brown sugar
    1 tablespoon parsley, chopped
    1 tablespoon chives, chopped
    ¼ cup flour, sifted
      Salt to taste

1. Wash, peel, and grate sweet potatoes.
2. Brown butter. Add sesame seed oil.
3. Mix sweet potatoes, sugar, chives, flour, and salt.
4. Make into two-inch patties, ½ inch thick. Or drop mixture, by the heaping tablespoon, into the hot, browned butter mixture, one-half inch apart.
5. Fry until golden brown on all sides.

Tomato-Pineapple-Peanut Salad

Tomatoes are a favorite Filipino vegetable and are combined with almost any other vegetable in hot dishes and salads. Although peanuts are not as commonly used in Filipino dishes as they are in Indonesian dishes, this salad particularly appeals to me since peanuts are essential to my diet!

    7 medium tomatoes
    1½ teaspoons powdered chicken base (or salt to
        taste)
    1 cup pineapple, diced and drained
    ½ cup celery, sliced very thin, at an angle
    2 tablespoons of your favorite salad dressing
        (Russian, French, Italian, or Roquefort)
    ½ cup peanuts, chopped
      Watercress or lettuce

1. Peel tomatoes.
2. Dice one tomato and combine with the chicken base, pineapple, celery, and dressing.
3. Slice remaining tomatoes, crosswise, 3 or 4 times, but not quite through.
4. Chill tomatoes and filling thoroughly.
5. Just before serving, add peanuts.
6. Spoon filling in center of each tomato.
7. Place tomatoes on bed of watercress or lettuce and serve.

Banana Fritters

The banana is just about the most popular fruit on the islands. Other popular fruits in the Filipino diet are papaya, mango, cantaloupe, watermelon, avocado, and pineapple.

      4 bananas
      1 cup flour, sifted
      2 teaspoons baking powder
      3 tablespoons sugar
      1 dash of salt
      1 teaspoon grated lemon peel
      ¼ cup aromatic rum
      ½ cup milk
        Oil to cover bottom of frying pan

1. Peel and slice each banana into 4 diagonal pieces.
2. Sift flour, baking powder, sugar, and salt.
3. Add lemon peel, rum, and milk. Mix thoroughly.
4. Heat oil in frying pan at medium heat.
5. Dip banana pieces in batter and fry until brown on both sides.
6. Serve hot or cold, plain if served with main course. When used as a dessert:

   (a) Sprinkle with powdered sugar that has been kept in a tightly closed jar with a vanilla bean.

   (b) Cover with a sauce made by heating ½ cup orange marmalade and 2 tablespoons Cointreau.

   (c) Or cover with a sauce made by heating ½ cup guava jelly and 2 tablespoons of aromatic rum. If you really want to gild the lily, sprinkle with grated coconut that has been crisped in the oven.

7. May be reheated by placing fritters in a 400° oven for approximately 5 minutes.

I wish I could include recipes for some of the delectable dishes of other major ethnic groups, such as the famous kim chee of the Koreans and the bean soup and sweet bread of the Portuguese, but I don't want to turn this into a cookbook at this stage. On the other hand, since *haoles* are the biggest ethnic group in Hawaii, I'm going to take the liberty of adding my favorite *haole* recipe from *Villa Montaña Cuisine,* which contains recipes from many countries.

Shrimp a la Villa Montaña

This is a buffet specialty at the Villa. With it baked ham is usually served and, among other good things, a green bean salad with Villa Montaña salad dressing. (If you want the recipe for the salad dressing and other Villa Montaña specialties, you can get them by sending $2.40 to Villa Montaña, Apartado 233, Morelia, Michoacán, Mexico, for a copy of *Villa Montaña Cuisine.*)

    6 deviled eggs (12 halves)
    ½ pound mushrooms and stems, sautéed
    1½ pounds cooked, peeled shrimp (if large, cut
        in halves or thirds)
    3 slices bread, diced, and browned in butter

Arrange eggs in buttered shallow baking dish. Cover with mushrooms and then cover with shrimp. Pour the following sauce over the top:

    4 tablespoons butter
    4 tablespoons flour
    2½ cups milk
        ½ to 1 cup grated American cheese, to taste
        Salt
        Pepper

1. Melt butter. Add flour, salt, pepper, and milk. Cook until thick.
2. Melt cheese in sauce.
3. Pour over shrimp mixture.
4. Place the diced and browned bread on top of casserole and bake until well heated, about 20 minutes at 350°.

If you're in Hawaii and want to learn to cook in any language, just watch the newspapers for announcements of cooking classes. Everyone but the Hotel and Restaurant Employees Union seems to be giving them.

If you're like me and don't care to cook and don't have to, it's not hard in Hawaii to find someone (at least a restaurant cook) to feed you in almost any language.

I have decided not to say anything in this chapter about alcoholic beverages, except that if you don't like my Mai Tai recipe in Chapter 5, or even if you do, try a Chi Chi (with a taste of coconut) at your favorite bar in Honolulu or sample the house specialties. You'll find good drinks despite outlandish names like Hotel Street Sweetheart, Test Pilot, No-Mo-Pain, and Pearl Harbor Punch.

PART

II

HAWAII'S MAJOR ISLANDS

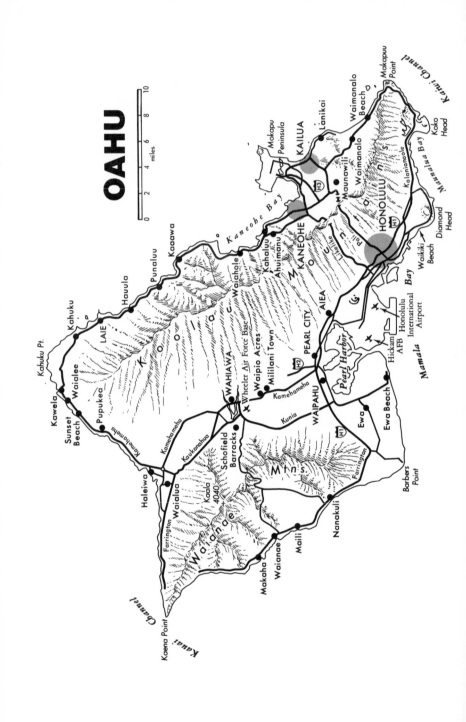

OAHU

miles
0 2 4 6 8 10

Kaena Point
Kauai Channel
Kaena Point
Farrington
Waialua
Haleiwa
Kamehameha
Pupukea
Sunset Beach
Kawela
Waialee
Kahuku Pt.
Kahuku
Laie
Hauula
Punaluu
Kaaawa
Kaneohe Bay
Waikane
Waiahole
Kahaluu
Ahuimanu
Makapu Peninsula
KAILUA
Lanikai
Waimanalo Beach
Makapuu Point
Kailui Channel
Koko Head
Kailua
Mokapu Peninsula
Waianae
Makaha
Maili
Nanakuli
Barbers Point
Ewa Beach
Ewa
Farrington
WAIPAHU
Kunia
Kamehameha
Waipio Acres
Mililani Town
Wheeler Air Force Base
WAHIAWA
Schofield Barracks
Kaukonahua
Kaala
4040
Waianae Mtns.
Koolau Range
Kaneohe
KANEOHE
Mauka
Nuuanu
Pali
Likelike
AIEA
PEARL CITY
Pearl Harbor
Hickam AFB
Honolulu International Airport
Mamala Bay
HONOLULU
Waikiki Beach
Diamond Head
Kalanianaole
Waimanalo
Maunawili
Kaneohe Bay
H1
H2
H3
H1

Oahu: The Gathering Place

Like a magnet, Oahu attracts islanders and Mainlanders. A curious blend of old and new, fast and
slow, beauty and ugliness. You'll love it or hate it.—
Anonymous.

Oahu in Hawaiian means "The gathering place." That is apt,
for on Oahu you'll find the greatest concentration of visitors, as
well as four out of five residents of Hawaii.

The island is small, about 40 miles long and 25 wide. Its area of
about 600 square miles makes it one-half the size of Rhode
Island. The population is under 700,000. Legally Oahu is part of
the City-County of Honolulu, which includes many small
islands.

Physically, Oahu is a mixed tropical salad. Downtown Honolulu resembles other tropical U.S. cities, except for its Oriental overtones. Waikiki resembles Miami Beach in many
respects. The rest of the island comprises two scenic mountain
ranges (highest peak 4,040 feet) with a green valley between.
The coastal areas are marked with rocky cliffs, sandy beaches,
and photogenic bays, plus military installations, suburbia, and
drowsing villages. In the rural sections pineapple and sugar
cane dominate the scene.

Almost everything I have previously said about Hawaii ap-
plies to Oahu—in many cases, especially to Oahu. Now I would
like to point out items of especial interest as you make an
imaginary tour of the island. (The best maps I have found for
touring Oahu are in *The Illustrated Oahu Tripmap,* published by
Island Heritage Limited.)

Let's assume you have just arrived from the Mainland by jet
plane and you are at the passenger terminal of the International
Airport.

GETTING DOWNTOWN

The scene in the modern open-air passenger terminal confirms that you really are in Hawaii. If friends meet you, they'll do so with flower leis and aloha kisses. Otherwise, you can buy a lei from one of the many vendors, if you need it to get into the Hawaiian mood. Lei or no lei, the mood is there in the tropical fragrances and foliage, the Hawaiian music that's almost bound to be playing, and the striking mixture of attire and ethnic groups that you'll find only in Hawaii.

Unless you're putting up at a nearby hotel or with friends, you'll probably claim your baggage and travel by bus or taxi to Waikiki.

En route you'll first pass through one of Oahu's least attractive areas: waterfront, industrial, commercial. A landmark is the 100,000-gallon water tank that resembles a giant pineapple —just to reconfirm that you are in Hawaii. This is the biggest pineapple of Dole's cannery (which it tops), the largest fruit cannery in the world. (Tours are available at a price.)

Soon you'll come to downtown Honolulu, where we'll pause for a look around.

DOWNTOWN HONOLULU

Honolulu, the center of business, government, education, and tourism for the state, is sometimes called the Crossroads of the Pacific. The downtown area is the heartbeat of it all.

The landmark of downtown Honolulu, although it is now overshadowed by skyscrapers, is the Aloha Tower (once the tallest structure in Hawaii) on the waterfront at Pier 9. From the free observation balcony on the tenth floor you can view the city and harbor—an excellent place to get your bearings.

Getting one's bearings in Honolulu requires learning that directions are not referred to as points of the compass. The direction from where you just came—toward the airport—is not called west but Ewa (an area beyond the airport). Eastward toward Waikiki is referred to as Diamond Head (after *the* natural landmark of Oahu, an extinct volcano just beyond Waikiki). Seaward is *makai*. The opposite direction, mountainward, is *mauka*. It takes a bit of getting used to, but you will learn it sooner than you think.

Near Aloha Tower you'll see freighters tied up at the piers, maybe even a passenger liner or two. And you'll see a unique ship, the *Falls of Clyde,* at its permanent berth, Pier 5. This partially restored, four-masted, fully rigged, sailing ship, now a museum, is said to be the only remaining one of its kind. At the turn of the century it plied between Hilo and San Francisco. In 1963, Hawaii's people bought it by popular subscription just before it was to be sunk to serve as a breakwater in Vancouver.

At adjoining Pier 6 is the red and gold restaurant ship *Oceania,* where diners may choose between Chinese and American cuisines in an elegant Oriental setting.

Looking mountainward (*mauka,* remember?), you'll see downtown Honolulu. The commercial center of town is the Fort Street Mall, a commendable contribution to the renewal and preservation of a business area, which, like those of many Mainland cities, was deteriorating, a victim of suburban shopping centers. The restored area is a spacious, restful pedestrian walkway with appropriate plantings, fountains, benches, and music. It is flanked by modern stores and office buildings.

Surrounding the Mall are some well-designed office buildings, but in unrestored areas, particularly in the Oriental and honkytonk section, dilapidated structures predominate.

In recent years the downtown section has enjoyed a resurgence with steady construction not only of business buildings, particularly in the financial district, but also of apartments, so that an increasing number of people who work downtown will live there and, to the joy of the merchants, shop there. There is a master plan of rehabilitation, which, if fully carried out, will cure most of the downtown ills and attract an ever-increasing number of shoppers. Lamentably, for the foreseeable future, parking will remain a problem despite a steady increase in parking facilities.

On the fringe of downtown is the State Capitol area, site of the old and new governments. An effort is being made to preserve historical landmarks in this area and maintain a parklike atmosphere through legislation to impose building restrictions, especially with regard to height.

A good way to see downtown Honolulu is to take a walking tour. Here is a partial list of downtown and near-downtown places of interest.

State Capitol. An open-air, no-entrance-door, architectural gem that seems to float on reflecting pools that symbolize Hawaii's role as the island state. No guided tours but great meandering.

Iolani Palace. The only former royal palace in the United States. Seemingly under perpetual restoration. Free. (Sign on nearby grounds reads "Caution: Walks slippery when flowers fall.")

Kawaiahao Church. Honolulu's oldest, once the royal chapel. Sunday services in Hawaiian and English.

Mission Houses Museum. Three historic buildings full of mementoes of missionary days. Admission charge.

Chinatown. Try the shopping tour sponsored by the Chinese Chamber of Commerce. Includes fascinating stores, food markets, and (for an added charge) lunch.

FROM DOWNTOWN TO WAIKIKI

The short drive along the coastal route (Ala Moana) encompasses a view of historic Fort Armstrong. Soon, and more interesting to me, comes Kewalo Basin with a seafood restaurant and a fleet of sightseeing boats, including a pink catamaran, a glass-bottomed boat, a large sailboat or two for dinner sailing, and yachts that daily carry sightseers by the hundreds to Pearl Harbor and other places of interest, with emphasis on the events of December 7, 1941.

Then appears spacious Ala Moana Park, with varied recreational facilities for all the family, and its seaward extension, Magic Island, for fine swimming and surfing.

On the opposite side of the street is Ala Moana Center, a gigantic shopping center that bills itself as the world's most interesting shopping center. I won't quarrel with that description. Almost everyone in Hawaii shops there at some time or other; I go mostly to sightsee.

WAIKIKI

Beyond Ala Moana Center you'll cross the Ala Wai Canal to Waikiki, the most famous beach resort in the world—the goal of millions of tourists.

Looking seaward, you'll first pass the Kaiser Foundation Hospital and beyond it the docks of the Ala Wai Yacht Harbor.

Next is a luxury condominium apartment-hotel, the Ilikai, the illustrious beginning of hotel row.

After the small garden-type Waikikian Hotel, if you turn right on Kalia Street, comes the sprawling complex of the Hilton Hawaiian Village. From there, except for a gap afforded by Fort De Russy (a military rest and recuperation center with its own beach), hotels and other tourist-oriented establishments stretch all the way to the Honolulu Zoo, which adjoins Kapiolani Park at the edge of Diamond Head.

Inland from the beach in Waikiki are hotels and apartment houses reaching to the Ala Wai Canal, which separates Waikiki from the Ala Wai public golf course.

Waikiki is made up mostly of hotels, apartments, shops, restaurants, beaches, people, cars, and buses. Some say that it is more: a state of mind that distinguishes Waikiki from other tropical resorts of its magnitude. Even when crowded, as it can be in the peak summer months, Waikiki seems to suffer less from congestion and frenzy than do other major beach resorts I have visited. Everyone seems to blend into the scene, minding their own business in a leisurely fashion, and wearing a smile. (Sign at entrance to parking lot: "Hello. Smile.") Most people are remarkably quiet. Hawkers are non-existent. A paperboy's call of the afternoon final edition sounds out of place.

That is not to say that Waikiki is not lively; far from it. There is action on the beach and beyond: swimmers, surfers, catamaraners, sunners, and gazers. At seaside veranda bars, barflies fly; on the sidewalks of Kalakaua Avenue and side streets strollers stroll; and in the many restaurants, ranging from standup snack bars to the regal place that advertises itself as the most beautiful restaurant in the world, diners eat food that is almost always good at prices for the most part surprisingly pleasing.

At night, garages and parking lots fill up, and locals join with visitors to enjoy a wide variety of nightlife. Some of the floor shows are of the Las Vegas variety, but more common by far are indigenous entertainers and rock groups (as of this writing).

I am sorry to add that nightfall brings out prostitutes (downtown in the honkytonk sections, too), purse snatchers, holdup men, and burglars. (I hope to be able to strike this paragraph from subsequent editions of this book.)

If you come to Oahu to live and need temporary, or even permanent, quarters, don't reject Waikiki out of hand as being too expensive. But if you go inland a block or two, as my wife and I have done on several occasions while sojourning on Oahu, you'll find some attractive, well-operated hotels and apartment-hotels with reasonable rates. Caution: Gauge the calibre of the management and your fellow-occupants before making any long-range commitments.

Among the sights to see at Waikiki are:

Hawaiian Wax Museum. Scenes from Hawaiian history realistically portrayed plus a notable collection of mementoes of the old days. Admission charge.

Bing Crosby's Hawaii Experience. Hawaii of yesterday and today in color on a 180-degree screen with stereo sound. Admission charge.

Waikiki Aquarium. Forty tanks of exotic fish plus seals, turtles, and collections of shells and coral from the Pacific. Children free.

Hawaii Calls. This long-running radio broadcast, which most of us have heard on the Mainland, originates at one hotel or another on Saturday afternoons. Free unless you make reservation for luncheon.

Kapiolani Park. Beyond the zoo, at the edge of Waikiki, are 200 acres of parkland containing facilities for sports from archery to polo, a bandstand for Sunday concerts, and the Waikiki Shell for musical events. Here the free Kodak Hula Show is held several mornings each week. Of this show one pollee commented: "Crass commercialism." Another: "I couldn't believe this wonderful show was free." Across the road on the ocean side are a park and beach patronized more by local families than by visitors. In this area is the Memorial Natatorium for swimming and swimming meets.

Some residents say they go to Waikiki only when they have visitors. A stock comment: "It's so touristy!" True. But many of us like Waikiki despite the touristy aspects, and to some extent *because* of them.

RESIDENTIAL HONOLULU (OTHER THAN WAIKIKI)

I would like to pause now on our imaginary tour of Oahu to mention the other residential areas of Honolulu, because that's where many newcomers live. A prospective new resident might profitably take a series of bus trips through Honolulu's residential areas that stretch from sea to mountains. On a bus, one doesn't have to give attention to driving and can therefore spend more time looking at neighborhoods. I won't try to rate the areas as to relative desirability; there's too much difference in tastes and purses.

Here I will list some of the attractions of interest. You can spot most of them on maps in the giveaway publications obtainable at the Hawaii Visitors Bureau, 2285 Kalakaua Avenue, or in hotels.

Bishop Museum and Kiliolani Planetarium. World's finest collection pertaining to the Pacific area. The planetarium features shows of the Polynesian skies. Admission charge.

Queen Emma Summer Palace. Royal Hawaiian relics. Admission charge.

Royal Mausoleum. The Kamehameha and Kalakaua dynasties are buried here.

Foster Botanic Gardens. Tropical trees, plants, and flowers, notably orchids. Free.

Liliuokalani Gardens. For picnicking near a waterfall. Free.

Moanalua Gardens. Nicely landscaped acres. Private but open to the public. Free.

Hawaiian Paradise Park. Birdland. Performing tropical birds with incredible antics. Admission charge.

Kamehameha Schools. Two hundred acres of highlands; hundreds of Hawaiian *keikis* (children).

Punahou School. The private school of Hawaii. Nicely landscaped grounds. Night-blooming cereus.

University of Hawaii and East-West Center. For viewing relaxed education that is a sight to see: the most colorful campus in America. East meets West in architecture, curriculum, and people.

National Memorial Cemetery of the Pacific. In this crater of an extinct volcano are buried about 22,000 veterans. Ernie Pyle's grave is the most frequently visited.

DIAMOND HEAD TO MAKAPUU POINT

If you continue past Kapiolani Park along the coast, you'll pass some elegant hotels, apartments, homes, and the Diamond

Head lighthouse before turning inland just a bit through a residential district. Then the road runs close to the sea again along Kahala Avenue before making a left turn inland at the Waialae Golf Course. (If you don't turn, you will end at the luxurious Kahala-Hilton Hotel.) Turn right at the first opportunity and you'll head again for the coast and the residential districts of Aina Haina, Niu, Kuliouou, and Hawaii-Kai.

The landmark on your right is Koko Head (elevation 642 feet); on your left is Koko Crater (elevation 1,208).

After you enter Koko Head Park, I suggest detours to Hanauma Bay Beach Park (beautiful and extraordinarily good for picnicking, swimming, snorkeling) and Halona Blow Hole Lookout (superlative seascape). Then comes Makapuu Point, the easternmost point of Oahu.

MAKAPUU HEAD TO KANEOHE

Shortly after turning north, you'll run into Makapuu Beach Park, a favorite of expert surfers. On the left side of the road is a favorite of everyone, Sea Life Park, a commercial offshoot of the Makapuu Oceanic Institute, which conducts oceanic research nearby. Billed as an oceanic adventure, Sea Life presents visitors with an opportunity to see how scientist-divers work, how porpoises can be trained to assist the divers, how a false killer whale can be induced to jump more than 20 feet into the air, and (the hit of the show) how a girl can ride a porpoise.

Offshore you'll see two small islands. Both are bird refuges and *kapu* to visitors.

After passing more beach parks, you'll turn inland to by-pass Bellows Air Force Base (inactive). If you like, you can enter the base for a picnic or swim on a fine beach.

Past Bellows you'll pass through a village or two and see the town of Kailua to the right. Turn right when you come to Route 61 (Pali Highway), and you'll enter Kailua, an attractive town, particularly the portion along Kailua Bay. At the beach, turn right on Kalaheo Street for Kailua Beach Park, one of the most attractive on Oahu. Beyond it is the Mid-Pacific Country Club, open to the public on weekdays for a greens fee.

Retracing your route on Kalaheo Street and continuing on that street, you'll come to the turnoff to the Kaneohe Marine

Corps Air Station, the Kaneohe Yacht Club, and the town of
Kaneohe. Kaneohe, Kailua, and their suburban sprawls house a
mixture of local business people, retirees, military and civilian
personnel of the air station, and commuters who work on the
other side of the island.

KANEOHE TO KAHUKU

Heading north from Kaneohe along the coast on Route 83,
you'll soon come to Ulu Mau Village, where for an admission
charge you can view a replica of an old Hawaiian village,
complete with indigenous gardens, and demonstrations of Hawaiian songs, dances, and crafts. At the nearby Heeia Kea Boat
Harbor you can take a glass-bottomed boat cruise to see some
enchanting coral formations.

Side trips in this area (save them for another day) include
Haiku Gardens, an old *kamaaina* estate that is lovely to tour.
Lunch is optional, but is, in my opinion, one of the finest buys in
the islands. Nearby and very impressive is the Byodo-In Temple, a replica of a beautiful temple in Kyoto.

Near the end of Kaneohe Bay, not far offshore, you'll see a
small island called Chinaman's Hat, because it looks like one.

If you have lunch in mind, the Crouching Lion Inn and Pat's
at Punaluu just up the road are very pleasant indeed. An alter-
native is to picnic at Kaaawa (yes, that was 3 a's) Beach Park,
Swanzy Beach Park a little farther along just before the town of
Punaluu, or at Hauula Beach Park just before the village of
Laie.

Laie, which has been described as Salt Lake City with palm
trees, was founded by Mormons. Here the Mormons have built
an imposing Temple, they operate a university, and they have
created a miniature Polynesia called the Polynesian Cultural
Center. I won't give you details of the latter; suffice it to say it is
a major attraction worthy of a full day's visit.

Just north of the Cultural Center, if you look sharp, you'll
spot a road to the right that, after some turns, will bring you to
Laie Point, which in my book (pun intended) affords the most
spectacular view to be found on the island.

Back on the highway, the next town is sleepy Kahuku, once a
sugar mill center.

KAHUKU TO HICKAM

From Kahuku, Route 83 turns westward and inland past the Kuilima Resort Hotel and golf course through the cane fields to Kawela. Between the two towns and a little northward is Kahuku Point, the northern extremity of Oahu.

After Kawela the highway runs in a southwesterly direction past several villages and some of the finest beaches of Oahu— Sunset Beach and Waimea Bay. The last beach park along this stretch is Haleiwa Beach Park, splendid for picnicking or camping.

Beyond the town of Haleiwa you could turn west on Route 99 and drive to Kaena Point, the westernmost point of Oahu, or turn southeast on Route 99 or 82 (which later joins 99) through the valley that lies between the Koolau mountain range to the east and the Waianae range to the west. Going south on either highway, you'll pass through more sugar cane and then through the world's largest pineapple-growing area. If you're lucky, the roadside stand may be open so you can try some fresh fruit.

Near the geographic center of the island is the town of Wahiawa, and nearby are Schofield Barracks, an Army installation, and Wheeler Air Force Base. Continuing south on Route 99 you come to Pearl City, whose economic pulsebeat is generated by the sprawling Navy Yard just south of it at Pearl Harbor. Near Pearl Harbor you can continue east into Honolulu on the freeway (H-1) or switch to Route 90, which will take you within a jet's roar of Hickam Air Force Base. Hickam shares runways with the International Airport, so now you're back about where you started your circuit.

You could have gone west at Pearl City on Route 90 or H-1 and, bypassing Barbers Point Naval Air Station, turned north along the western coast of Oahu, which is strewn with villages and beach parks. The paved road ends at a military reservation shortly before reaching Kaena Point, the westernmost tip of Oahu. This journey along the coast is a scenic one: inboard rises the Waianae mountain range; outboard slope some of the finest beaches in Hawaii, including the Makaha beach, home of international surfing meets.

The tour I have described is similar to those offered by sightseeing companies, hospitable hosts, and, surprisingly often, by casual acquaintances resident in Hawaii. With it behind us, at least in mind's eye, I'll turn to some of the facts of life on Oahu.

THE A TO Z OF OAHU

AA. You're not seeing double. But if you were, it might be useful to know that Alcoholics Anonymous exists in Alohaland and can be reached by phoning 537-1030.

AAA. The triple-A (American Automobile Association) also functions on Oahu and, if you are a member, will give you a helpful sightseeing book.

Agriculture. As is apparent from what I have already said, Oahu has many facets. A shining one economically is agriculture. Forty percent of the land is zoned for agricultural use. Pineapple and sugar are the big crops. In addition several diversified agricultural products make up surprisingly high percentages of the state's total production.

Art. Art in Hawaii runs the gamut from Polynesian and Oriental to Pop and Op. On Oahu you can see it all in galleries ranging from the sedate Honolulu Academy of Arts to the Saturday and Sunday Art Mart, where 50 island artists display their work on the zoo fence.

The venerable Academy of Arts is truly the art center of Hawaii. Its 29 galleries and 5 inner courts occupy nearly a city block and house an enviable collection of Oriental art and Western art ranging from ancient to contemporary. Most of the Italian and French masters of the Renaissance are represented, along with modern artists of renown.

Knowledgeable islanders combine frequent visits to the Academy (special exhibits always, including an annual exhibit by artists of Hawaii) with lunch in its small, inviting Garden Cafe. The cafe, operated by volunteers under the supervision of long-time Academy member M'Lou Watumull (whose culinary expertise I learned of long ago, when we were friends in India), offers superb soups, sandwiches, and desserts. Call 538-3693 for a reservation.

For what's going on at the galleries, consult the "Coming Up" page in the *Sunday Star-Bulletin*. And for art courses consult the Academy of Arts and the Bishop Museum.

The "fence" art mart is a thing apart. It stretches and

stretches, but still has a waiting list of artists who would like to show there. Arthur Murray (*The* Arthur Murray) lives nearby and lends his promotional expertise. Here's a sample ad: "Shopping for new paintings along the Zoo Fence is like attending a gay, happy festival. Look over the assortment of beautiful Hawaiian paintings in glowing colors. You'll enjoy chatting with the friendly artists—some of Hawaii's finest painters. Take home a picture on approval. See how it can make your room come alive. Come this Saturday—9 to 4 P.M. Save 25%!" Small wonder Murray has sold millions of dance lessons.

Oahu has many "name" artists, some as colorful as their canvasas. I haven't space for much name-calling here, but I'd like to mention two artists who are often in the news.

Jean Charlot was a prominent muralist in Mexico before he moved to Hawaii. I haven't met him, but we have mutual friends among artists in Mexico. This industrious, civic-minded man must never sleep. His works, many monumental, I have seen all over Hawaii. In his spare time he has written at least eight books and, in the Hawaiian language, plays.

Margaret Keane's artistic ability was long hidden behind that of her artist husband, who for years was credited with distinctive pictures of round-eyed children—I'm sure you've seen them. After a marital rift, it came to light that Margaret had painted them. She has her own gallery now in the Sheraton-Waikiki Hotel.

Beachboys. What would a book on Hawaii be without a mention of those Waikiki landmarks (seamarks?), beachboys. Some say they are a dying breed. The ones I see look healthy.

Beaches. Next to pineapples, what Oahu seems to have the most of is beaches. My list of beach parks totals 47. And there are miles of good beach not incorporated into parks—at Waikiki, for instance. In only about half of the beach parks is the swimming officially rated as good. But the parks don't exist just for swimming. They may include basketball courts, picnicking and camping facilities, playgrounds, etc.

Surfing is a big thing on Oahu. My list of surfing areas totals 51. Some are safe only for experts.

Scuba diving is popular, too. I have a list of 22 areas, mostly at their best in the summer.

Drownings on Oahu beaches are not uncommon. Moral: Never swim without a lifeguard or expert swimming buddy present!

Boat Docks. Dock space is in short supply. Moral: Don't sail to Oahu without prior arrangements. You may write to the Harbors Division, Government of Hawaii, 700 Fort Street, Honolulu, Hawaii 96813.

Calendar of Daily Events. The newspapers carry lists of non-commercial events each day as a public service.

Camping. Residents and visitors are fortunate to have many public camping grounds in parks. Camping is free but by permit only. Otherwise, too many people would camp permanently to escape the high cost of housing. Camping grounds are closed in January.

For complete camping information, you should obtain the brochure, "Have Fun Safely on Oahu's Beach Parks." Write to Department of Parks and Recreation, 1455 South Beretania Street, Honolulu 96814.

Churches. Listings of Oahu's churches fill up four pages of the Yellow Pages.

I would like to add here that non-sectarian services are conducted on Sunday mornings in the chapels of several Waikiki hotels. The Waikiki Beach Chaplaincy conducts services on the beach at the Hilton Hawaiian Village. Buses marked "Church Bus" provide service from Waikiki to Honolulu's major churches each Sunday morning.

Clubs and Organizations. If you're a joiner, chances are good that on Oahu you'll find your favorite excuse for a night out, or a three-martini lunch, or an afternoon away from the home or office.

The Yellow Pages classify the listed organizations (two pages of them) as: Aviation, Business, Civic, Educational, Farm, Fraternal, Health, Labor, Medical, Political, Relief, Religious, Veterans', Welfare, and Young Peoples'.

Crime. Crime is a serious problem on Oahu, more so than on the Neighbor Islands.

An anti-crime war is being vigorously waged on Oahu by a concerned government and an energetic, enlightened police department. Measures meeting with some success include the use of police helicopters, a campaign to engrave social security numbers on expensive pieces of personal property, foot patrols in Waikiki, and television cameras to scan the public areas of banks.

Even if the crime wave continues, it is reassuring to read the ending of crime reports such as one I received: "We had a robbery involving over $250,000 in household silver and jewelry, plus the world's finest collection of early United States silver dollars. The latter were retrieved by ransom in such manner as to provide a plot for Hawaii Five-0. The cooperation of the police, and especially the detectives who gave even their free time to protect our property and family during this operation, deserve our praise."

Ecology. Of all Hawaii, Oahu has suffered the worst at the hands of the despoilers of nature. Waikiki, not long ago lined only with low buildings compatible with the palm trees and the sea, has become another Miami Beach architecturally, to the sorrow of old-timers. Raw scars from building and highway projects mar the island. Ill-advised housing developments contribute to unwarranted traffic congestion, floods, and facility shortages. Hope for improvement is found in an aroused populace whose efforts are spearheaded by ecology-minded organizations.

Entertainment. Entertainment for most Oahu residents is mostly where they find it: at home, in a neighbor's home, in the park, on the beach, at a church luau (the cheapest kind).

When residents feel the urge for commercial entertainment, they find a bountiful variety. Here are some of the offerings:

Concerts. The Honolulu Symphony Orchestra is the big sound, offering a subscription season at the Honolulu International Center and other concerts. The Royal Hawaiian Band provides free concerts on Fridays at noon in the Iolani Palace Bandstand and at 2 P.M. each Sunday in Kapiolani Park. Visiting musical talent lends variety throughout the year.

Nightclub and Restaurant Shows. After sundown, Waikiki is synonymous with entertainment. Perennial favorites are Don Ho and Hilo Hattie. New entertainers come and go in profusion. I can't keep track of them. You can, if you're so minded, through the entertainment sections of local newspapers and the several giveaway publications that cover this field.

Spectator Sports. For baseball, it's the Islanders of the Pacific Coast League. For football, it's the World Football League. For basketball, the University's teams get the big play, but at the high school level also you can see fine football at times. In early January the Hula Bowl attracts top college players annually. The list of other spectator sports and their protagonists is too long for these pages—consult the sport pages of local papers.

Theatre. Best theatrical bet is the federally endowed Hawaii Performing Arts Company. The Honolulu Community Theatre and the Theatre for Youth present several productions each year. At the University, in the John F. Kennedy Theatre, classical and modern productions are presented by the Department of Theatre and Drama. Tickets to the University plays are hard to come by. And on the windward side of the island, the Windward Theatre Guild offers good theatre. Professional Mainland companies visit from time to time.

Fishing. Fresh-water fishing may be enjoyed at the commodious Wahiawa Public Fishing area. Consult the Hawaii Visitors Bureau for details and for information on ocean fishing.

Golf. New golf courses blossom on Oahu so fast that I'm not sure how many there will be when you read this. Not counting those under construction, I know of 26 at this writing. Of these, nine are open only to military personnel and their guests. Of the others, all but two or three are open to the public, at least on weekdays.

You may obtain the latest information on Oahu's courses from the Hawaii Visitors Bureau.

Government. The City-County is administered by an elected mayor and nine-member Council. They do a pretty good job, considering the problems that beset them and the difficulties of working with the state government, which never gives Oahu as much money as it would like.

Hotels. Hotels are pushing out the coconut trees in Waikiki, but are scarce elsewhere on Oahu.

There is no cutthroat rate-cutting. Oceanview rooms in the de luxe hotels come high, as they do at all resorts. Bargains exist for those who persist in shopping around. A newly arrived resident or prospective resident would do well to obtain from the Hawaii Visitors Bureau a copy of its annual publication,

Hawaii Hotel Guide, which has descriptions and prices of hotels statewide.

Housing. On Oahu, where building lots are scarce, a three-way squeeze is on. Ecologists don't want agricultural and undeveloped land converted to home sites. Aesthetes don't want more high-rise high-density units such as those that now blight Waikiki and other areas. Home-seekers—a rapidly increasing group—don't want to continue to be balked by scarcities and unreasonably high prices. In Chapters 7 and 8, I dealt with housing and the quest for it throughout Hawaii. Here just let me add, "Good Hunting!"

Hunting. If it's game rather than housing that you're looking for, you stand a sporting chance on Oahu for wild pig and fowl, but hunting on the Neighbor Islands is less chancy.

Libraries. In addition to the downtown library at South King and Punchbowl Streets (near the Capitol), the state operates numerous branch libraries and bookmobiles on Oahu. I have visited many of Hawaii's public libraries and find that they need not take a back seat to those on the Mainland; many excel in imaginative displays; most excel in services and courtesy to patrons.

Medical Facilities. According to experts with whom I have talked, medical facilities on Oahu are equal or superior to those of similar areas on the Mainland. The Honolulu County Medical Society has a grievance procedure to handle patients' complaints.

The island has more than 20 public and private hospitals. For the military, Tripler Army Hospital offers 1,000 beds.

Military. In these days when military personnel can often choose their place of assignment, I can't think of a better place than Oahu for servicemen to enjoy a tour of duty. Let me list some of the bonuses available to them and their families.

1. Housing or housing assistance to help beat the cost of living.

2. About 10 officers' open messes and an equal number of NCO messes for variety and economy of dining out.

3. Post exchanges, base exchanges, and Navy exchanges; five major ones and many branches.

4. Four well-stocked commissaries.

5. Nine military golf courses.

6. Numerous military beaches (with cabins at Bellows and at Wainae Army Recreation Center).

7. And to get away from it all, on the nearby island of Hawaii at 4,000 feet near the edge of a volcano, is a de luxe facility, Kilauea Military Camp, where the motto is "Everyone a VIP."

Newspapers. The major newspapers are the *Honolulu Advertiser* (morning) and the *Honolulu Star-Bulletin* (afternoon). The address of both is P.O. Box 3350, Honolulu, Hawaii 96801. They publish a combined paper on Sundays.

Radio and Television. Almost twenty AM and five FM radio stations are on the Oahu air. Four commercial television stations are supplemented by the educational station, KHET.

Restaurants. Many pollees commented that the way to save money in Hawaii is to stay out of restaurants, especially in Waikiki. True, true. But I like to eat in good restaurants now and then, and I'll bet you do too (as interested in saving money as we both might be). One thing especially nice about dining out in Honolulu is that you can eat in almost any language.

My dining experiences on Oahu have been, almost without exception, pleasurable. Ordinarily my wife and I frequent neither the most nor the least plush establishments. We have found that, in general, prices on Oahu, including Waikiki, are no higher than they are in large Mainland cities for comparable food, service, and ambiance.

I have already mentioned a few restaurants and I shall now mention a few more. But lest I be accused of playing favorites, I'm simply going to list in alphabetical order the dozen Oahu restaurants most frequently mentioned in response to my question, "What restaurants do you especially recommend?"

Canlis'	One of Waikiki's best.
Chuck's Steak House	Four Waikiki locations.
Bistro	Gets raves from residents.
Haiku Gardens	A luncheon favorite on the windward side.
La Ronde	Round and round you go. Sunday brunch.
Maile	In the Kahala Hilton. Very popular with residents.

Michel's	Like the Maile Room, a frequent Holiday magazine award winner.
Pagoda	"Floats" on waters brilliant with carp.
Pearl City Tavern	Seafood, steaks, Japanese food. Japanese decor. Monkey bar with 35 live ones.
Reuben's	Steaks, lobster, chicken. All good.
Top of the I	Atop the elegant Ilikai Hotel.
Willows	Garden place noted for coconut cream pie.

Shopping. I've dealt with this subject here and there, mostly in Chapter 8. Here are a few suggestions that may add spice to your shopping on Oahu.

1. Check out the downtown area on foot. The Fort Street Mall affords pleasant walking and shopping, as do the surrounding streets. And don't overlook the Chinese and Japanese shops. Melva buys tea (including rose tea) at the Tai Yen Company and medicinal herbs from herbalist (and accupuncturist) Setwin Tang, both on Maunakea Street.

2. Allot as much time as you can as soon as you can to browsing the Ala Moana Center. Watch the people, particularly the *keikis*. Put on your shoes (if you've removed them) and ride the escalator to the second level and watch the carp being fed. Look closely at the architecture, plants, flowers, fountains, and sculptures. Visit the aviary. Talk with sales clerks. Lunch at a snack bar—in Japanese or Chinese perhaps—or in one of the elegant restaurants. Shop if you must. You'll have a choice of giant emporiums such as Sears, J. C. Penney, Woolworth, Liberty House, and M. McInerny, Ltd.; a supermarket such as you've never seen, chock full of foreign foods; a Japanese department store; two big drug stores; and enough specialty and service shops to bewilder a country boy like me.

3. Get acquainted with other shopping centers around the island, including the visitor-oriented King's Alley and International Market Place in Waikiki.

4. Browse the mini-shops and galleries that abound.

Tennis. Tennis on Oahu, as on the Mainland, is increasing in popularity. Hardcourt facilities (like those in California) abound. An increasing number of free public courts are lighted. For details, consult the Department of Parks and Recreation.

Tourism. Like the military presence, tourists will always be with you on Oahu unless (heaven forbid) pollution drives it away. Be thankful for tourism; it adds interest to life on Oahu.

Transportation. I covered motorized transportation in Chapter 7, particularly from the cost angle. Here I'm going to mention two inexpensive modes that are popular today on Oahu, and one that should be one of these days.

Bicycling is being practiced and talked about widely these days, not as recreation for children but as serious transportation for all ages. Agitation grows for a network of bicycle paths. Forecast: An early system of bicycle paths.

Walking (hiking, if you like) is good for wallet and waistline. If you'd like to get off the beaten path in safety, get in touch with the Hawaii Trail and Mountain Club.

Planning is underway for a mass transit system, but details must await a subsequent edition.

Youth. Oahu, particularly Waikiki, is burdened with irresponsible transients, many of whom are shy, gentle young people. Some, unfortunately, are the opposite, especially when on drugs, as the newspaper crime reports attest.

Waikiki's main street, Kalakaua Avenue, suffers also from an invasion by a quite different type of youth. I refer to the saffron-robed young members of the Hare Krishna cult, who impede sidewalk traffic and assault the ears of shopkeepers and pedestrians with their monotonous tambourine-accompanied chanting, which is permitted by the police on the grounds that it is a devotional service. I wonder what would happen if all of the other religious sects of Hawaii decided to hold services in this free space?

Young and old of Oahu work together to provide recreational facilities. In city parks, close to 20,000 youngsters participate in summer programs, which are sponsored by the Department of Parks and Recreation and staffed with employees and hundreds of volunteers, junior and adult.

In Kuhio Park Terrace, a low-rent development with a reputation that could bear improvement, an athletic program sponsored by a variety of organizations, including the police, is improving behavior patterns.

I could go on and on, but I'm sure you've gotten the message —youth on Oahu has its hangups as on the Mainland, and Oahu is facing up to them.

Zoo. I promised to end up with *Z,* so here we go to the zoo at the far end of Waikiki. Admission is free as I write this, but some think that a small admission fee to help defray rising costs would be in order. Did you know that an elephant eats 100 pounds of food a day? The Honolulu Zoo has two elephants and a lot of other animals with big appetites.

This isn't the greatest zoo in the world by any means. Still, the people-watching animals and the animal-watching people draw me again and again. I hope you can be among the many thousands who not only visit the zoo but also enjoy "happy hour" entertainment while picnicking there on summer evenings.

WHAT RESIDENTS LIKE AND DISLIKE ABOUT OAHU

I won't take up much space with the *likes,* because they largely parallel the *likes* about Hawaii that I reported in Chapter 4. Such things as climate and recreational facilities, for example, rate high with Oahu residents. I am going to quote here comments on just two subjects: public servants and drivers.

"The courtesy of the civil service—from police department to tax collectors is a striking change from the Mainland. So far, Honolulu hasn't had Mainland-style police assassinations; no race riots either. The entire relationship of public servant to private citizen is in better balance."

"Countless times we are impressed with the courtesy of the drivers—letting people turn left, park, etc. One never sees this in Michigan, let alone thinks of doing it himself. Now I find myself letting people ahead, etc."

As for *dislikes,* here are some quotes from pollees:

"I don't like the indifference shown consumers by most retail and service businesses" (college student).

"Too small a community." (He last lived in Tokyo.)

"Appalling rush hour traffic."

"The generally low class behavior of some minority groups in school, initiating violence and other behavior not acceptable in a 'gentle' society."

"Condition of cars (brakes and lights) is poor compared with

California, for example.''

"Incredibly slow building rate on much needed highways contributes a great deal to poor driving conditions.''

"Noisy cars.'' (May I add: and motorcycles and trucks.)

"Termites can be a problem.''

"The high cost of living'' (the most common complaint).

"Tourists.''

"The drivers—a majority of them—who consistently exceed the speed limits.''

"The expense of traveling off the island.''

Now here are some miscellaneous gripes culled from interviews, conversations, newspaper articles, and letters to the editor.

Abandoned Cars. They are still a familiar sight, but the state now has a program that permits owners of unwanted cars to call the police for free removal. The army has a program, too, for cars abandoned on its property. A helicopter picks them up and dumps them on an artillery range for cannon fodder.

Dead Animals. Dead animals in public places headed the list of complaints received by the Mayor's office of information and complaint, according to one of its quarterly reports.

Massage Parlors. The publisher of a giveaway magazine complained in one issue that, "When you go into one of these joints, they ask your name. If it's not in their file, a massage is all you get. If it *is* on file . . . well, you can take it from there.''

Falling Coconuts. The cautious or frugal homeowner doesn't include coconut trees in his landscape planning. If he does, and if he doesn't keep them trimmed (or maybe even if he does), and a coconut falls (as they often do) and bops a guest on the head, the homeowner might be in for a lawsuit. That is why coconut tree trimmers do a nice tree-trimming business at $10 a tree in private and public places. I think it's the near-misses that people complain about most, and no one has collected *yet* for a near-miss.

Television Commercials. Hawaii's television stations sometimes run in extra commercials, thus making useless the time schedules published by the local media. When a fellow's expecting to see a football game and instead gets another ten minutes of a cooking demonstration, he's tempted to do a little demonstrating himself.

WRAP-UP

Don't get the mistaken idea from reading the gripes on the last few pages that residents of Oahu would prefer to live elsewhere, say, on the Neighbor Islands or California. No. It's clear to me that most share the sentiment of E. Alan Holl, an architect, formerly of Marin County, California, who told me, "All's not paradise, but it is a wonderful place to live and raise a family."

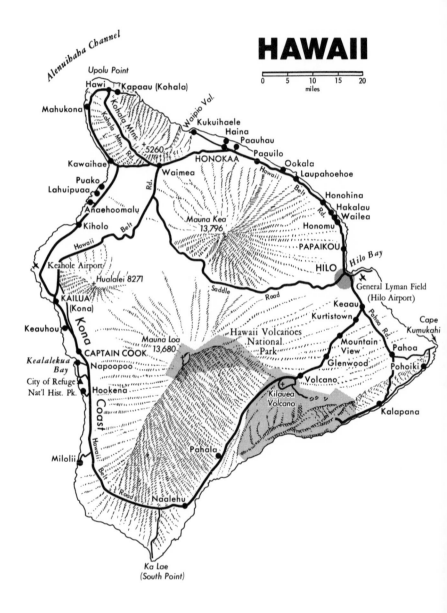

HAWAII

miles
0   5   10   15   20

Alenuihaha Channel

Upolu Point

Hawi · Kapaau (Kohala)

Mahukona

Kohala Mtns.

Kohala Mtn. Rd.

5260

Waipio Val.

Kukuihaele

Haina
Paauhau

Paauilo

HONOKAA

Ookala
Laupahoehoe

Waimea

Kawaihae

Puako
Lahuipuaa

Anaehoomalu

Hawaii

Belt

Honohina
Hakalau
Wailea

Kiholo

Hawaii

Belt

Mauna Kea
13,796

Honomu

PAPAIKOU

HILO

Hilo Bay

Keahole Airport

Hualalai 8271

Saddle

Road

General Lyman Field
(Hilo Airport)

KAILUA
(Kona)

Keaau
Kurtistown

Cape
Kumukahi

Keauhou

Kona

Mauna Loa
13,680

Hawaii Volcanoes
National
Park

Mountain
View

Pahoa

Pahoa Rd.

CAPTAIN COOK

Glenwood

Pohoiki

Kealalekua
Bay

Napoopoo

City of Refuge
Nat'l Hist. Pk.

Hookena

Coast

Volcano

Kilauea
Volcano

Kalapana

Milolii

Hawaii

Belt

Pahala

Road

Naalehu

Ka Lae
(South Point)

Hawaii: The Big Island

Some people do not like this island. It's much a matter of temperament, but for me this is the blessed jumping-off place to the Happy Hereafter.—E. Earl Glass, now in his eighties, who came here in the fifties.

The island of Hawaii has three apt nicknames: the Big Island, the Orchid Island, and the Volcano Island.

Residents prefer the nickname the Big Island. By Hawaiian standards it is big—almost twice as big as the other islands put together. By Mainland standards it is small, four-fifths the size of Connecticut. Its population is small by almost any standard, around 70,000.

Hawaii is called the Orchid Island because it boasts more than 22,000 varieties of orchids. Hilo, the county seat, is the center of the state's orchid-raising industry.

The name Volcano Island is inevitable, because Hawaii was formed by five volcanoes, three of which are champions. Kilauea and Mauna Loa are the most active in the world. Mauna Loa is the world's largest active volcano and, with a visible land mass of 2,000 square miles, it is also considered the largest single mountain in the world. Mauna Kea, if measured from the ocean floor, is the world's highest mountain. Mauna Kea and the other two are considered dormant.

Hilo (population 29,000) is the only city in the state other than Honolulu that is connected with the Mainland by commercial flights. Inter-island flights connect Hilo, Kailua-Kona (a major tourist area), and Waimea-Kahala (a ranching and tourist area) with the other islands of the state.

With that brief introduction, I would like to take you on an orientation tour of this highly diversified island. (The Hawaii Visitors Bureau can supply you with a fine map without charge.) We'll start in Hilo and go clockwise, taking a quick look at some of the highlights.

Hilo is a verdant town, charming and uncrowded. Architecture is a compatible mixture of old and new. The waterfront along Hilo Bay was severely damaged by tidal waves in 1946 and 1960. What remains of the old downtown section is mostly of yesteryear, but the new civic center is a pleasing combination of green parks and modern buildings. Nearby is spacious Liliuokalani Gardens Park with Japanese-style landscaping. It is flanked by a hotel complex on the bay.

Hilo doesn't boast of its high rainfall, an average of nearly 140 inches. It is the wettest city in the state, but as the visitors bureau will point out at the drop of a drop, much of the rain comes in heavy rainfalls at night. Many of the days are rainless or with only a trace. The visitors bureau says: "If we didn't have the rain, we wouldn't have the flowers and lush tropical growth that visitors expect to see."

Hilo does have flowers galore! Not only orchids but also anthuriums, ginger, and bird of paradise are grown for export. Hibiscus, the state flower, doesn't travel well, but can be seen in more than 5,000 varieties in gardens and along the roads. My wife and I never fail on a visit to Hilo to stop by one of the nurseries and buy an exotic arrangement or two to mail to the Mainland by air—surprisingly cheap and unsurprisingly welcome gifts.

From Hilo, Route 11 takes us southeast past the Lyman Field Airport. Eight miles out, we switch to Route 13 for a side trip to the Puna district, which occupies the eastern corner of the island. It is a haunting area of black sand beaches, largely-undeveloped subdivisions, tropical rain forests, and lava-flows dating from as far back as 1750 to the present decade. As recently as 1960, a village was buried by cinders. In one respect this is the fastest-growing area in Hawaii: the coastline was extended considerably by the 1959 lava flow.

Until a few years ago, one could continue through this area to the center of Hawaii Volcanoes National Park. Now the road is closed after it enters the park, owing to recent lava flows, so one must backtrack to Route 11 to reach the craters of Kilauea.

I won't add to the millions of words that have been written about this area except to say that it attracts thousands of residents of Hawaii, as well as a multitude of Mainlanders, when Kilauea erupts. Locals from all over the state rush *to* the fiery spectacle, *not* away. In hot weather this is a favorite vacation area for residents because of the cooling 4,000-foot elevation.

Continuing south from the crater, we'll descend to the Kau district, mostly a desert region of black sand beaches and lava rock that occupies the southern part of the island. A new condominium complex and golf course foreshadow what is to come.

Near the southern tip, the southernmost point of the United States, you can view a monkeypod tree said to have sprung from the roots of one planted by Mark Twain in 1866.

The landscape of the southwest corner of the island is dominated by lava flows dating back to 1868. Housing subdivisions border the highway. North of the lava flows we'll come to a historic stretch of west coastline that includes the City of Refuge, a National Historical Park marking the site of an ancient sanctuary for lawbreakers. It is reported that in recent years a fugitive from Mainland justice sought refuge there in vain. When the police caught up with him, they said, "Tell it to the judge." Melva and I, too, once took refuge there—from the noonday sun. Under a tree on the edge of the sea we combined picnicking with fisherman-watching.

A bit farther north is Kealakekua Bay. Captain Cook landed here a year after his first landing on Kauai and again a month later. The second landing was his undoing. The natives decided he wasn't a god, as they had thought, and killed him during a melee. A commemorative monument marks the spot.

And now we enter coffee country, where the famous Kona coffee grows on the slopes of Mauna Loa, and a mill is open to visitors.

We will pass through a succession of villages, predominantly Japanese and Filipino, and turn left toward the coast at the first opportunity on Kam Road. This brings us to the Kamehameha development project on Keauhou Bay, where the golf course and housing development will eventually (maybe) be surrounded by nine hotels.

Continuing northward along the ocean, we pass through a residential area. We could stop for a swim at Kahaluu Park or the tiny White Sands Beach, which is also known as the Disappearing Sands beach because at times its sand washes out, exposing the lava base. When Melva and I swam at White Sands, the sand was there, but Frisbee-throwing hippies and swimming dogs limited our enjoyment of the fine swimming.

We are now in the so-called Kailua-Kona area (directly west of Hilo). On or near Kailua Bay are about a dozen hotels, most of them in the luxury class, and several of what I call, for lack of a better term, shopping centerettes (clusters of small shops, ice cream parlors, snack bars, offices, and what-nots in one building. It is a historic area. Witness the Hulihee Palace, which was built in 1838 with walls three feet thick and then remodeled into a summer palace for King Kalakaua in 1884. It is now operated as a museum by the Daughters of Hawaii. Across the street stands the Mokuaikana Church, built by the missionaries in 1823, possibly the oldest church building in the islands. Inland are houses, apartments, and business establishments.

Just north is the modern airport. Beyond that is the partly-completed coastal highway to be lined with beach parks and hotels and residential developments all the way north to Laurence Rockefeller's Mauna Kea Beach Hotel, rated as one of the world's finest.

What makes this west coast area so popular is the dry weather, with temperatures dropping and rainfall rising as the terrain rises toward Mauna Kea volcano. The Kona Chamber of Commerce says that the Kona coast enjoys the fiftieth state's most consistent and pleasant weather, and upon the basis of my several sojourns there I wouldn't quarrel with that statement. And the scenery and sunsets are spectacular.

Driving north from Kona, we switch to Route 19, which will take us to and across northern Hawaii, passing through the Waimea-Kamuela area and its tremendous Parker Ranch, and then southeast down the coast through the sugar cane and a series of villages, to Hilo.

The Parker Ranch is often described erroneously as the largest privately owned ranch in the United States. The King Ranch in Texas is bigger. To me the impressive statistic about the Parker Ranch is the fact that it supplies a fifth of the beef consumed in the state.

At Kamuela, the heart of the cattle country, we could have made a scenic detour on Route 26, passing near the Mauna Kea Beach Hotel, to the somnambulant northern tip of the island that slopes down from the Kohala mountains (highest point 5,500 feet), but I'll save that for you to explore on your own (I hope) some day.

The center of the island, except for a rough and narrow ridge road from Hilo to near the Waimea Kohala airport, is not highly recommended for cars. This area of the volcanoes is of interest principally to hunters, hikers, and scientists.

THE A TO Z OF THE BIG ISLAND

Agriculture. The state of Hawaii is the largest producer of sugar among the states of the Union, and the island of Hawaii is the largest producer among the islands of the state. That makes sugar production the largest industry on the island. Cattle ranching ranks next; half of the beef raised in the state comes from the Big Island. Hogs and poultry round out the animal husbandry. Two-thirds of the fruits grown in the state, excluding pineapple, and one-third of the vegetables come from here. Kona coffee, exotic flowers, and macadamia nuts round out the agricultural picture.

Art. In Hilo, art galleries come and go. When you arrive look for the list in the weekly *Orchid Isle*. In the Kailua-Kona area you'll find art works for sale in the hotels and shopping centerettes.

Beaches. The island has close to twenty beach parks. Some beaches have white sand, some black, and there is even a green sand (crystals of olivine) beach. The black sand was made by hot lava that exploded into bits when it hit the ocean and was further pulverized by time and tide.

Camping. Camping is permitted in many parks, but don't count on it near Kailua-Kona, where hippies so abused the nearby facilities that they had to be closed.

Churches. The missionaries landed here first. Now old mission churches vie with Buddhist temples for visual attention. A dozen or more denominations can be found. Consult the Yellow Pages.

Clubs and Organizations. Major mainland clubs have their counterparts here. If you can't find your favorite in the Yellow Pages, ask the Chamber of Commerce.

Crime. Crime is not a big problem on the Big Island. I've seen newspaper ads offering rewards for the arrest and conviction of Parker Ranch cattle rustlers; I've read of scattered arrests of nude bathers (most of them scatter when police approach); and I know that raids on cockfights are habitual on weekends.

Crimes against visitors are abhorred by the local people. When a soldier was beaten and robbed, the Chamber of Commerce took up a collection to reimburse him. How's that for civic action?

Most of the criminals are not vicious. When a policeman spotted three men carrying marijuana plants down the road, he used his handcuffs to secure one, then borrowed a piece of cord from him to secure the others, all in a line.

Ecology. The Big Island is relatively free of the pollutions that afflict most of the Mainland. The air is smoked up by cane burning here and there, but the people have learned to live with that. The sugar industry says that there is no way as yet to eliminate the burning of the canefields after the harvest and at the same time enable the industry to survive economically. The problem is being attacked, and I think it is just a question of time until there will be no more cane burning.

As for water, I've heard no complaints of ocean water unfit for swimming. True, until recently sugar cane wastes were dumped into the ocean. That practice ended with the construction of a power plant fueled by such waste. The new plant will supply about one-fifth of the island's electricity needs.

As for visual pollution, there has been reasonably good control over construction so far. The failure of speculative subdivisions to develop has led to suggestions that subdivision lots on which no buildings are constructed within five years of purchase should revert to the state. To reduce speculation, which leads to uneven development of a subdivision and unsightly vacant lots, it has been suggested that a covenant should run with the land to prohibit each successive titleholder from reselling it before placing some improvement on it.

Education. The island has 30 public and 9 private schools. In Hilo is the only four-year branch of the University of Hawaii; also there is a two-year community college affiliated with the University. Pollees' comments about schools were included in Chapter 10.

A school with a short history and a long name is Ke Anaina o ka Hoomana Hawaii Ponoi, designed to perpetuate Hawaiiana by reviving the culture of the ancient Hawaiians. Open to all races, the school seeks to attract Hawaiian children. The curriculum includes weaving, farming, growing and use of herbs, arts, crafts, the Hawaiian language, and even fishing.

Employment. The watchword for newcomers is caution. Here are the words of the local Chamber of Commerce: "Before any decisions are made to relocate here, we strongly advise you to come and investigate thoroughly. We have a critical employment problem and an acute housing shortage and the cost of living is higher than most parts of the country."

As in all of the Neighbor Islands, so in Hawaii the most likely source of employment for newcomers is in tourist-oriented businesses. Anyone contemplating setting up a business should consult with the Chamber of Commerce.

Entertainment. Most of the hotels in Hilo and Kailua-Kona offer after-dark entertainment. The "happy hour" is a common institution. Piano bars abound. Most shows cater to tourists and have a Polynesian motif with Hawaiian music and hulas.

Live theatre is furnished mostly by the Kona Coast Players

and the Hilo Community Players. Occasionally, road shows by the University of Hawaii or other groups reach the island.

Commercial motion picture programs are supplemented by regular filmings at the libraries.

Residents entertain themselves with such activities as archery, bowling, square dancing (at least three clubs), lawn bowling, and bridge (duplicate weekly at Hilo and Kona).

Fishing. Famous marlin (billfish) fishing grounds are only an hour's run off the Kona coast. This is the site of the colorful annual Hawaiian International Billfish Tournament, termed by some locals the billfish and beer tournament because of the vast quantities of beer consumed at dockside during the event.

As for fresh water fishing, a prawn caught in the Wailua River was measured and weighed at the courthouse one day: 26½ inches and 14½ pounds.

Golf. I can count nine golf courses; more are under construction. The Robert Trent Jones course at the Mauna Kea is one of the world's most prestigious courses. I wish I could say that the Volcano Golf Course lies not more than a fairway drive from the crater, but that would be a lie—two miles would be a closer figure. The municipal course at Hilo is my favorite—cheap and friendly. Where else are sixsome's welcome?

Government. The county has an elected Mayor and a nine-member County Council with four-year terms. It is one of the few governmental entities I know of that sometimes has a surplus of funds.

Hotels. With few exceptions, hotels are concentrated in Hilo and Kailua-Kona. They range from modest ones that Melva and I have stayed in, such as the Dolphin Bay in Hilo (friendly management, excellent housekeeping units, free bananas) and the Kona Sunset (mahimahi with macadamia nuts an outstanding dining room specialty), to the top-bracket Mauna Kea Beach (finest buffet lunch I've ever had) that I'm getting a little tired of mentioning.

Housing. Newcomers are faced with few vacancies and high prices. Hilo is the most likely place to find rental housing at anything approaching reasonable rent. Rents approximate those of Oahu. Advertised houses rent from $250 and up; two-bedroom apartments from $150 and up plus utilities. Rooms without kitchen privileges or private bath range upward from $60 a month.

Prospective buyers may fare better, but should count on paying at least $30,000.

In the Kailua-Kona area most of the vacant units are occupied by their owners during part of the year, and therefore unavailable for permanent residents. Prices tend to be higher than in Hilo.

Hunting. Wild pigs and goats roam in public hunting areas. There are bow-and-arrow seasons for wild sheep. Bird hunters bang away from November to January at pheasant, quail, partridge, and doves.

Industry. Sugar milling is the biggest industry. Agriculture supports an expanding food-processing industry. Hardwood timber is being increasingly used by sawmills for flooring, eventually perhaps for plywood. Diversified manufactures include sportswear, heavy equipment, concrete block, and brick. A preferred new industry is research and development. Physical features such as the volcanoes and deep ocean waters offer advantages for research in astrophysics, geophysics, and oceanography.

Konane. Sometimes called "Hawaiian checkers," this ancient game may be played with lava pebbles and coral fragments on the stone outdoor board in the City of Refuge. Or you can do as Melva and I do: play with bottle caps and a board drawn in the sand with a stick. Or you can play in the comfort of your home with checkers on a checkerboard.

The game is simple (I usually lose). Here are the rules, less some of the unnecessary protocol. Fill all the 64 spaces on a checkerboard (you can have more spaces on a homemade board if you wish) alternatively with contrasting markers. Checkers are fine, but one set won't provide enough markers. Make sure all the markers in each *diagonal* row are the same color. The red player (assuming you have red and black markers) removes one of his markers from the center or a corner of the board. His opponent then removes one of his that is immediately adjacent to the empty space. The red player now jumps a black marker and removes it. (Jumping may be multiple but in only one direction at a time and never diagonally.) It is now the black player's turn to jump with one marker, and so on, until one player finds that he has no marker to jump and thus becomes the loser. Welcome to the club!

Libraries. The main library is in downtown Hilo. It is supplemented by ten branches and bookmobile service.

Macadamia Nuts. My wife told me I'm not mentioning enough things of particular interest to women. To which I replied, "Nuts!" To which she countered with "Great! Tell them what to do with macadamia nuts."

All right. The first thing to do with macadamia nuts is to save up enough money to buy them. These little golden nuggets cost me $1.35 in Hilo for a 5-ounce can or jar. They're no cheaper at the Hawaiian factories and can be more expensive at specialty shops. They are crispy and crunchy and are delicious with predinner drinks, if you don't fear calories. But that isn't what my wife wanted me to tell all you ladies out there. She wanted me to tell you that macadamia nuts can be used with tasty results in place of almost any other nuts called for by your favorite recipes. Here's a nutty one from the producers of Royal Hawaiian Macadamia Nuts that Melva and I think is very smooth:

Silken Soup

    1½ cup well-seasoned chicken broth
     1 ripe banana, thinly sliced
    ½ teaspoon curry powder
     2 teaspoons dry sherry
    ½ teaspoon fresh lemon juice
     1 egg yolk
    ¼ cup whipping cream
       Snipped fresh chives
    ¼ cup macadamia nut bits

1. Combine broth, banana, and curry powder in a saucepan. Bring to a boil and simmer for 5 minutes.

2. Turn into a blender container and whirl until smooth. Add sherry and lemon juice and whirl a bit more.

3. Beat egg yolk with cream and, with blender speed set at low, gradually add cream mixture to broth. Whirl until smooth.

4. Chill thoroughly.

5. To serve, ladle into small pots or bowls, sprinkle lightly with chives and macadamia nuts. Serves three or four.

6. This soup can also be served hot. After whirling in the blender, return it to the saucepan for reheating and serve hot, with garnishes. May also be made earlier in the day and reheated at serving time.

Medical Facilities. The medical center of the island is Hilo Hospital with 360 beds. Four smaller hospitals serve outlying areas. The Department of Health operates various clinics for eligible residents.

Military. The only major military installation is the Kilauea Military Camp, a rest and recreation center in the Volcanoes National Park, for military personnel, families, and guests. If you're not military and receive an invitation, don't fail to accept it.

Newspapers. The *Hawaii Tribune-Herald* is published daily in Hilo. Its tourist-oriented *Orchid Isle* comes out weekly. On the Kona side is a bi-weekly, *West Hawaii Today.*

Another giveaway, the *Hawaii Island Guide,* provides visitors and residents with a calendar of events, basic information, and feature articles of local interest. Mrs. Helene Hale, the publisher, speaks with authority: she has served as Mayor of Hilo, as County Commissioner, and now is president of an advertising company.

Radio and Television. The island has four radio stations and is served by satellites of Oahu's television stations and by cable television.

Restaurants. When dining out, most residents join the tourists at the big hotels. For instance, Sammy Amalu, the Honolulu columnist, gave a dinner party at the Orchid Isle of which he said, "They served a meal that I would never have believed possible in the more or less bucolic environs of the Big Island. It was fantastic."

I've never eaten at a Hilo hotel, but a resident, the artist Emrich Nicholson, took Melva and me one evening to a little unpretentious restaurant in Hilo named Roy's Gourmet. Good Japanese and American dishes at fantastically cheap prices.

Some of my Hilo friends are enthusiastic about Dick's Coffee House in the Hilo Shopping Center for good food at good prices.

In the Kailua-Kona area, it's a different story. Some of the many hotels serve fine food, e.g., the buffet lunch at the Kona Inn is popular with residents. Melva and I have had good dinners at the Kona Sunset. As to restaurants, the moderately priced Oceanview and the Hukilau are favored by residents as well as tourists. Melva and I have dined well at Huggo's, near the Hilton. The Billfisher Inn has individual thatched-roof dining rooms, a friendly bartender, and what are said to be the prettiest waitresses in town.

Senior Citizens. The Hilo Senior Citizens and the Kona Senior Citizens meet regularly. Melva and I once attended a meeting of the latter group—a lively bunch, I tell you.

Shopping. The largest shopping center on the island is Kaiko'o Hilo Mall, an enclosed, air-conditioned complex housing about 25 businesses. The biggest stores are Kress, J. C. Penney, and Mall Foods. (The latter gives customers a directory of items and corresponding shelf numbers.) Nearby in the Hilo Shopping Center you'll find Sears, Ben Franklin, Pick & Pay Super Market, and others. The biggest store in the old downtown section is Woolworth.

Food prices in Hilo are competitive, because several large supermarkets are concentrated within a small radius. In two major downtown stores I priced the eleven items that I had priced on Oahu a couple of weeks earlier. The total costs varied widely. In one store the cost was the same as the cheapest store on Oahu; in the other the cost slightly exceeded that of the most expensive store on Oahu. So, if you shop for groceries in Hilo you'd better *really* shop.

Kailua-Kona has only one large supermarket. I was not surprised, therefore, to find that those same items there cost almost

11 percent more than the average in the Oahu stores (7% more than the higher of the two stores I shopped in Hilo).

Absence of competition in the Kona area is not limited to supermarkets. Many residents feel that more by design than happenstance they are forced to deal with one-of-a-kinds in many lines of business. What this does to prices you can imagine.

Skiing. Skiing on Hawaii's Mauna Kea is for the strong of heart: the elevation is around 13,000 feet and there are no lifts, no public lodgings, no warming huts, and sometimes not enough snow to make a snowball. The best snow is usually in February and March. When conditions are right, the skiing on runs up to three miles long, can't be beat. Skiing is permitted on Saturdays and Sundays only. To get there you need a four-wheel drive vehicle. Equipment can be rented in Hilo.

Tennis. I have a list of 15 places with tennis courts, most of them open to the public free. The Hawaii Visitors Bureau can supply details.

Tourism. The Big Island is a favorite of tourists for three reasons: jets to the Mainland, spectacular performing volcanoes, and weather-worryless Kona—no one wants a rainy vacation unless he's peddling raincoats on the side. Tourism dominates Kona; it touches Hilo mostly at the airport and the Banyan Drive hotel area.

Tourism, so I've been told, also disrupts marriages on island farms. The wives get jobs at the hotels and earn more than their husbands back at the farm. Husbands get suspicious of improvements in wives' dress and grooming. The wives get ulcers. The husbands get divorces.

Transportation. I've mentioned inter-island and island-Mainland air transportation. Cruise ships occasionally call at Hilo. County buses run from Hilo to Kailua-Kona and from Hilo to the southeast area.

The only other public transportation on the island is the so-called "sampan" busline in Hilo, which, for most residents and visitors, is something to see rather than to ride. Service is erratic and uncomfortable. Hitchhiking is prevalent.

Newcomers often rely on rental cars while they wait for their car to be barged in, or while they shop for one on the island. I've always been able to rent an almost-new Datsun or Toyota at a reasonable price. To get the best rate you may have to shop among the concessionaires.

Youth. The island has its share of young transients, but few serious problems have arisen from their presence. A notable exception was the shooting of two hitchhikers by a 23-year-old local man who admitted to police that he did not like hippies. One of the victims died, and the killer was sentenced to 30 years imprisonment (later reduced to 5 years, so I've been told) after he said he was sorry for what he had done.

Said the sentencing judge: "You may disagree with another man's sense of values . . . but he is a human being nevertheless —fully entitled to the protection of our laws. The life of a stranger in our society is just as sacred as the life of each and every member of our community . . . and the law must be upheld and enforced—in order that no man, woman or child in our community shall have to live in fear."

Zinnias. In addition to the exotic flowers I have mentioned, many so-called Mainland flowers grow here in profusion: roses, begonias, daisies, chrysanthemums, carnations, pansies, gardenias, marigolds, and *zinnias*.

WHAT RESIDENTS LIKE AND DISLIKE ABOUT THE BIG ISLAND

From questionnaires and other sources, it appears that, aside from the almost universal complaint about the scarcity of housing and the high cost of living, residents of the Big Island are a happy lot.

True, residents of Hilo don't (with some exceptions) care for the super-abundance of rain in that area. And true, many residents of the dry Kona area complain of too much tourism and too many hippies.

There is some complaint from both areas about the limited shopping facilities, but this is more commonly heard from residents of the Kona area, who say that a complete shopping center is needed, and in the next breath tell me that the small town atmosphere is one of the charms of Kailua-Kona.

Scattered complaints have reached me about medical facilities, noise, isolation, motion picture facilities, bugs, weeds, and the difficulty of obtaining repairs. Such gripes appear to be more than balanced by the commonly heard plaudits for the island's climate, people, beauty, informality, and pace.

WRAP-UP

A 35-year-old mother, who moved to Oahu for business reasons, wrote me as follows:

"We lived for a year on the Big Island. The people were so warm and generous that we had trouble paying for our meals. We'd eat in a small local place and find some anonymous person had paid our bill while we ate! A friendly attitude, with respect for others' customs can get you to many unforgettable places. Don't try to prove your importance—try to find out about others. Be willing to adapt yourself and to appreciate new foods, entertainment, sports." (No anonymous person ever paid for a meal for me on the Big Island, and I wouldn't count on it if I were you.)

The lady who was running the Welcome Wagon in Hilo told me not too long ago that of 36 new families that had moved to Hilo in a month and a half, 23 had come directly from the Mainland. She added that eight out of ten who come from the Mainland to the Hilo area return within two years. I understand that the return rate is lower in the Kailua-Kona area. Whatever the area—the watchword is caution. Don't move to the Big Island without a good look around first.

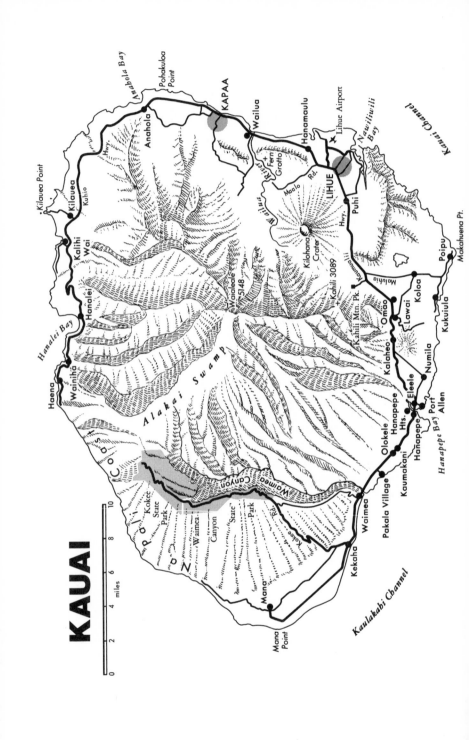

KAUAI

Kauai: The Garden Island

Life here is filled with beauty and peace. The only
problems one has are self-created.—Jeannie Boaz,
formerly of San Diego.

Kauai (pronounced Ka-WA-ee), aptly called the Garden Island, is lush with natural and cultivated vegetation. Rice pad-
dies, sugar cane, ferns, flowering trees, shrubs, and flowers
make it a horticulturist's dream come true.

Kauai might with equal aptness be called the island of con-
trasts. Let me give you some examples of what you'll find on
this small circular island (32 miles in diameter).

In the center is what may well be the wettest spot on earth,
Mount Waialeale, with an average annual rainfall of 486 wet
inches on its swampy top. Twenty miles away, the town of
Kekaha on the coast has less than 20 inches annually.

Gardens only a few miles apart feature, respectively, plants of
a tropical rain forest and desert succulents.

Some of the sleepiest villages imaginable drowse only a few
miles from a missile range.

Formed from a single volcano, Kauai is the oldest of the
Hawaiian islands and the first to be sighted by Captain Cook.
Kauai is the least developed and least populated of the main
islands—the least despoiled by man, Fewer than 31,000 people
live there, yet it offers visitors and residents modern amenities
in profusion.

I can't take you on a circle tour of Kauai, because the terrain
of the northwest corner, with help from conservationists, has so
far defied the roadbuilders. So let's suppose you have landed at
the airport on the outskirts of the county seat, Lihue (population
3,200). First, we'll drive through town and to the end of the
coastal road in the west. Then, retracing our steps, we'll drive

along the coast in the other direction to the end of the road. Having done that, except for some sideroads, we will have traversed all the highways of the island. The center, dominated by Mount Waialeale and lesser mountains, is of principal interest, aside from its natural beauty, to scientists, hunters, and hikers.

Lihue was largely rebuilt in the 1960's. The heart of the town today is the attractive Lihue Shopping Center and adjoining circular office building. Nearby are the post office, banks, and other shops. New residential developments have kept pace with the town's growth, and some colorful old buildings have been preserved and restored. New public buildings include a super-modern library, the Wilcox Memorial Hospital, a State Office Building, and the Kauai Memorial Convention Hall. On one edge of town is a growing industrial park.

Just south of Lihue is a bayside village called Nawiliwili, the principal port of Kauai. It is flanked by the Kauai Surf, an elaborate hotel complex complete with golf course and clusters of cottages on a bluff overlooking the bay. From Nawiliwili, suppose that, without returning to Lihue, we proceed via Route 58 to Route 50, the highway to western Kauai. A short detour would have taken us to the Alekoko Fish Pond, which is believed to pre-date the Polynesians. Some even say it was built by those legendary little people, the *menehunes*.

Once on Route 50, we see on our left the Hoary Head mountain range, dominated by the dome of Mount Haupu. On its slope, tour guides point out a profile of Queen Victoria.

On the right is Kahili Peak (5,170 feet), sometimes veiled in clouds, sometimes standing in sharp relief. Behind this is Mount Waialeale, the watershed of Kauai, the source of seven rivers.

When we come to Route 52, we'll turn left on it for a detour to Koloa and Poipu Beach. For the first half mile the road is lined with giant eucalyptus trees planted 65 years ago. To me, this shady avenue of greenery is one of the most restful sights in all Hawaii.

Koloa is a charming old plantation town with few marks of modernity. Its unchanged appearance is the result of design, not chance, and is made possible because all of the land belongs to one estate. The modern bank, supermarket, and post office will probably remain the only buildings out of character with the old wooden stores with iron roofs.

The story is different when you reach the beach. Here, where you'll find the best swimming and surfing on Kauai, inevitably you'll find new hotels, some of tasteful though modern design.

Poipu Beach Park offers calm waters and facilities. Nearby is Brennecke's beach, unexcelled for body surfing (surfboards are banned). My wife and I have sojourned in this area three times and plan to return again and again. The housekeeping units of the Poipu Shores Apartment-Hotel leave little to be desired in the way of amenities. One ocean-front apartment that we favor looks down on a rocky inlet virtually below the lanai. Toss down breadcrumbs and fish swarm up to fight for them.

Leonard, the owner-manager, must have a last name, but I never learned it. We were on a first-name basis from the moment he helped me with my luggage. When my wife tired of cooking, we feasted on Leonard's occasional offerings of such staple but tasty dishes as ham hock and limas or spaghetti and meatballs, or we cooked our own meat on the outdoor grill provided for the use of guests.

A dead-end road west from Poipu Beach takes us past Kuhio Park and to Spouting Horn, a come-and-go geyser created by waves forcing water through a lava tube on the shore. In this area is the Prince Kuhio Hotel with its Tahitian Longhouse restaurant, a scenic place to dine.

The public road ends just beyond Spouting Horn, so we'll return on Route 52 to Koloa, and there take a shortcut via Route 53 back to Route 50.

Mount Kahili still lies on the right as we pass through a rolling area of small farms and villages. All of this locality comprises McBryde Plantation (it was leased in 1860 by a Scotsman for a cattle ranch). Much of the area has been turned over to homesteaders.

When we come to the town of Kalaheo, we'll make a short detour by turning left just past the ballpark and driving for about a mile to Kukuiolono Park, once the home of one of the McBrydes, now a county park with a 9-hole golf course that is operated on the honor system. Golfers simply sign up and drop the modest greens fee in the box. Rental carts, hand and electric, stand nearby for rent on the same basis.

Back on the highway after our detour to the park we soon come to the historic Hanapepe valley and the towns of Hanapepe and Port Allen. Port Allen is a shipping center and was long the home of the McBryde Plantation's sugar mill. The next town is Kaumakani, a model plantation village. Then comes Waimea on Waimea Bay, where Captain Cook landed in 1778, and where later the Russians built a fort, the remains of which can still be seen. This was Kauai's early harbor and trading center.

At Kekaha we'll leave the coast, turn right through the canefields, and then up and up into the Kokee State Park and some of the grandest scenery anywhere. We can stop at several lookouts, each presenting a different panorama of the Waimea Canyon, which is often compared with the Grand Canyon of Arizona. I have visited both the Grand Canyon and Waimea Canyon several times. I wouldn't say that one is more beautiful and striking than the other. They both impress upon me how infinitesimal I am in nature's grand plan.

After the canyon we'll drive on to Kokee State Park, a rain forest with such contrasting elements as a missile range and a museum. Here also is Kokee Lodge, a complex of modern cabins, comfortable for a long or short stay.

At the end of the road is the Kalalau lookout, affording on a clear day a view of the Kalalau valley below and the sea beyond that for me is indescribable. Words like breathtaking, awesome, dramatic, and spectacular come to mind. Oftentimes, pity the luck, the view is obscured by mist.

On the way back down the mountain we will see tiny islands offshore, some uninhabited except by birds and rabbits. The largest, Niihau, is inhabited by about 300 people. Niihau is privately owned, and visitors are not allowed.

Upon our return to Kekaha, we could turn right and continue along the coast for a few miles. This area is called Barking Sands, because of the noise made sometimes when the sand here is compressed. It is a military reservation, but beaches are open to the public.

Now let's see what would lie ahead if we had gone north on Route 56 from the airport, rather than to Lihue and westward. After the villages of Kapaia and Hanamaulu, a side road takes us to Hanamaulu Bay and its public beach park. Soon on the right will appear the fairways of Wailua golf course, a sporty 18-hole layout operated by the county.

Just past the golf course, a road leads off to commodious Lydgate Park with extensive facilities along its mile-long beach and a salt water lagoon for swimming.

A turnoff just before the bridge spanning the Wailua River would take us to the Wailua Marina and the complex that serves as the setting for Paradise Pacifica (a 31-acre tourist attraction with a fine evening show) and as the launching area for boat tours up the river to a fern grotto.

These tourist attractions are popular with local people as well.

The turnoff just *across* the bridge spanning the Wailua River would take us upland to fine residential areas called Wailua River Lots and Wailua Homesteads. Here Opaekaa Falls drifts like a veil to a pool below.

On the main highway, just beyond the bridge turnoffs I have mentioned, stands one of the island's most popular hotels, the Coco Palms, located in what is said to be Hawaii's largest coconut grove.

Across from the Coco Palms is a popular bathing beach, and beyond it along the shore a string of hotels, apartments, and a shopping center, the Market Place.

Next comes Kapaa, the largest town on the island (population about 3,800). Kapaa hit a slump some years ago when a pineapple cannery closed, but the nearby tourist complexes are reviving it economically. Now it is a mixture of old and new, boasting a shopping center and a fine new library.

After Kapaa we'll pass two more drowsy villages, as Kealia and Anahola. Side roads lead to beaches, a rock slide, and tiny communities. On the left are the Anahola mountains. The road side is lined with cane fields and pasture land.

At Kilauea skirted by the highway we can turn right past a defunct sugar mill to the Kilauea Lighthouse with a fine view of the rugged coastline spread out below.

From Kilauea to the north end of the island, known as Hanalei, is a succession of seascapes and beaches, each an outstanding attraction. On the left is a turnout where one can pause for a view of the beautiful Hanalei valley with the river winding through it. Taro grows here today, but I'm told that during the gold rush of the 1850's, oranges were shipped from here to California. Beyond the lookout on the right the old Princeville Plantation is being developed as a tremendous housing complex with a 27-hole Robert Trent Jones golf course.

Soon the road drops sharply to the town of Hanalei, which stretches sleepily along the highway. The Waioli Mission here was established in 1835. Between the highway and Hanalei Bay are vacation homes and a fine beach.

Beyond Hanalei is much-photographed Lumahai Beach, where portions of *South Pacific* were filmed. The road ends a short distance beyond some small caves, which are wrapped in legends I shall not go into. The Kalalou Trail starts here. It leads to a view of some of the spectacular cliffs of the Napali coast and into a hiker's paradise.

THE A TO Z OF THE GARDEN ISLAND

Agriculture. Sugar is the No. 1 industry and the prime agricultural product of this island, the home of Hawaii's first successful sugar plantation. Nowadays a fifth of the state's crop is produced here. Mills convert the cane into raw sugar, which is dumped into a bulk storage plant on the edge of Lihue for transfer to ships in Nawiliwili harbor and thence to refining plants in California.

Pineapple used to be the island's second industry, but most pineapple acreage has been converted to cane fields because, it is said, of a losing competition with cheap foreign canned fruit.

Other principal crops are bananas and papayas. The corn seed industry is growing, as is the production of taro, now being promoted as a health and baby food. More than half of the state's taro is grown here.

Cattle raising is a thriving business, also.

Art. Galleries come and go. One that seems to have staying power and features local artists is the Spouting Horn Art Studio in Koloa, which displays the work of owners Elise and Frank Train. For other galleries, consult the Yellow Pages.

Beaches. I've covered this pretty well during our island tour. If you need more details, ask at the Hawaii Visitors Bureau in the Lihue Shopping Center. (The director, Maile Semitekol, is especially helpful and personable.)

Business Opportunities. Inquire at the Chamber of Commerce, upstairs in the Lihue Shopping Center. I'm sure that the manager, Fred Nenow, will be helpful.

Camping. Facilities at about 18 beach parks are generally excellent. If you don't own a tent and want to camp in the mountains, Kahili Mountain Park (a private enterprise) has fully equipped tents and cabins. They even wash your dishes for you! Mountain cabin camping is also available at Kokee State Park.

Churches. About fifty churches represent some fifteen denominations.

Climate. For my money the official publication is right. It says: "Kauai has an almost ideal climate with average temperatures near the coast of 71 degrees in February and March, and 79 degrees in August and September. Cooler temperatures in mountain areas such as Kokee offer a pleasant contrast. Rainfall varies widely depending on location."

Clubs and Organizations. I have a six-page list put out by the Chamber of Commerce, which can supply details.

Crime. Crime on Kauai makes so few headlines that when a camper was clubbed by two men, it made sensational news throughout the state. One resident told me that he laughs when he sees visitors locking their cars, but I have read of car lootings and burglaries, so I lock my car when on Kauai, as I do elsewhere.

Ecology. Kauai has few ecological problems. Cane burning, yes. It is hoped that a long-range development plan for the island will assure adequate control of future construction and land development.

Education. There are 14 public and 7 private schools on Kauai. The fast-expanding Kauai Community College offers liberal arts, career training, and community service programs.

Employment. Suitable employment for newcomers is probably more difficult to find on Kauai than elsewhere in Hawaii. Tourist-oriented businesses offer some opportunities.

Entertainment. For most residents, entertainment is enjoyed mostly on the beaches and in the homes. Commercial entertainment can be found in hotels, particularly on weekends. The swinging place for residents is the Jetty Club in Nawiliwili, where audience participation in the floor show is common and sometimes uncommonly good.

Fishing. Fresh-water fish, including trout, are stocked in some streams. Kauai also offers fine blue-water fishing. Bonefish and yellowfin tuna, both famous fighters, are among the several species that are caught in record-breaking sizes.

Golf. I have already mentioned Kauai's four courses. They offer enough variety to please almost everyone. Residents are especially pleased with the low greens fees available to them at the Wailua course.

Government. The mayor and seven-member County Council are elected for two-year terms. The county includes the island of Niihau and two tiny uninhabited islands.

Hotels. Kauai offers not only an abundance of luxury and near-luxury hotels for the visitor, but also, to a greater extent than the other Neighbor Islands, seems to have more modestly priced but adequate hotels of the type especially useful to newly arrived residents in search of permanent housing. Best to look them up in the Hotel Guide and look them over if you need one.

Housing. Like the Big Island, Kauai has a housing shortage that makes it difficult for newcomers to find suitable housing at anything like a reasonable price.

The newspaper ads are likely to prove disappointing in a search for rentals, and real estate men may throw up their hands helplessly in response to inquiries about non-luxury housing.

Buying or building offers better prospects than renting. I talked with Bob Prosser and Clint Childs of Prosser-Childs

Inc., the island's largest real estate brokerage firm. "Inventory," says Prosser, "is the problem. We sell it as fast as we get it."

Another enterprising realtor, "Robbie" Lear, head of Kauai Realty, Inc., told me over a cup of coffee that he solved his own housing problem by building a pre-fabricated home sent from the Mainland. Hicks Homes, which I have mentioned, has probably built more houses on people's lots than any other builder in the state. Driving around on Kauai, I have been impressed by the number of Hicks homes I saw, including many under construction.

Affluent Mainlanders can buy a piece of the multimillion-dollar resort Princeville at Hanalei, which offers building in a wide range of styles and prices.

Hunting. You can hunt wild pigs in some areas the year round on weekends. The bird and goat season is more limited.

Industry. Tourism is the island's biggest industry, if you include one without smokestacks. Manufacturing is largely confined to the processing of foodstuffs and the manufacture of garments. Fields in which expansion seems likely are forestry, fishing, and aluminum processing from Kauai's extensive deposits of bauxite, as yet untouched. Research and development by the federal government is expected to expand steadily.

Libraries. In addition to the fine library in Lihue that I mentioned, there are branch libraries in Kapaa, Hanapepe, and Waimea. A bookmobile serves outlying areas.

Medical Facilities. The Wilcox Memorial General Hospital in Lihue and the Kauai Veterans Memorial Hospital at Waimea are general facilities. In Kapaa the Samuel Mahelona Hospital with 110 beds is a tuberculosis institution that also treats mental and alcoholic patients.

Military. Approximately 100 military and 400 civilian personnel operate the Pacific Missile Range Facility at Barking Sands.

Museum. The Kauai Museum under the direction of Robert Gahran was a good one even before the "Story of Kauai" exhibit in an adjoining building came on the scene. Now the combination is outstanding. The new exhibit combines filmings from a helicopter of rare views, a diorama of Captain Cook's arrival, artifacts, photos, and other displays that will acquaint one with Kauai pleasurably and rapidly.

Newspapers. The only general newspaper is the twice-weekly *Garden Island,* which also publishes a monthly giveaway for visitors called the *Tourist Press,* which is useful to residents as well.

Radio and Television. Kauai has two radio stations. Television is relayed from the nearby Oahu stations. Cable TV is available in some areas.

Restaurants. Among the places in Kauai where I have enjoyed dining are the Plantation Manor—cold salad forks and plates, hot wet hand towels after dinner, personalized souvenir matches; the Waiohai Hotel—luncheon that couldn't be faulted; Reuben's—friendly service and fine food. Those places were all favored by pollees, as were the Hanamaulu Restaurant (Oriental food), JJ's Broiler, and Kenney's. Next time I'm on Kauai, I'm going to try them all.

Shopping. The Lihue Shopping Center is a well-designed and landscaped complex. A two-story circular building houses offices. In other buildings are some 15 businesses, including a Foodland Super Market (one of Hawaii's biggest food chains) and a Woolworth store.

The landscaping of the center follows Polynesian and Asian motifs. Fountains, ferns, flowers, and benches encourage shoppers to linger and visit.

The Rice Shopping Center, nearby, is smaller.

A small shopping center at Kapaa serves that area with a bakery, restaurant, supermarket, Ben Franklin, post office, and other businesses.

I shopped the two Lihue supermarkets and found that my market basket of groceries cost 5 percent more in one than in the other. The cost in the cheaper store was more than 12 percent higher than the average cost in Oahu stores for the same items.

Tennis. Tennis facilities are excellent at the Kauai Surf Tennis Club, the Kiahuna Tennis Club, and on public courts you'll find here and there around the island.

Tourism. Kauai, which is closer to Honolulu (flight time 27 minutes) than is Hawaii or Maui, attracts Oahu residents who "want to get away from it all," as well as out-of-state visitors. A growing emphasis is on conventions held in hotel facilities or in the County's War Memorial Convention Hall, which seats more than 1,000. The future of the visitor industry on this island looks rosy, indeed, if it can remain as unspoiled as it is today.

Transportation. Kauai is served by an air taxi service and by helicopters, as well as the scheduled inter-island airlines. There is an inter-island barge terminal at Nawiliwili and container freight facilities.

The buses of Smith's Transportation Company run hourly from Nawiliwili, through Lihue, past the golf course, major hotels, Kapaa, and on to Kealia, where they turn around and come back. Drivers will stop on signal.

Kauai does not prohibit hitchhiking, if it is done from the shoulder of a road.

Youth. Kauai is officially tolerant of youthful transients who behave themselves, but not of those who disturb the customs of the community.

Here are some pertinent extracts from a leaflet prepared in cooperation with the creative writing class of the Community College for the Kauai Chamber of Commerce and the Lihue Professional and Businessmen's Association.

"We invite you to share the wealth of beauty which abounds . . . to meet our friendly people . . . who, like people anywhere are apt to become disturbed if their tranquil community is threatened or marred. . . . You will be ignoring local custom by entering a store or public building dressed only in a bathing suit or shorts . . . nudity is not acceptable except in the privacy of one's home. . . . It is not the custom here to pick fruit without explicit permission. . . . Our policy is to arrest and prosecute offenders, whether for shoplifting or drug use. We try to provide full employment for local families which makes temporary jobs difficult for short term visitors to obtain. . . . The local attitude is that welfare support should be for the needy who qualify and not for the mentally fit and physically able bodied. . . . Kauai, which is said to be one of the last few remaining paradises in the world, deserves the help of each and everyone of us. . . . We sincerely hope your visit here is an enjoyable one."

Zonta. The last-listed organization on my list of clubs and organizations of Kauai is Zonta, an international business and professional women's club. It meets the first and third Thursdays at noon at the Kauai Surf Hotel.

WHAT RESIDENTS LIKE AND DISLIKE ABOUT KAUAI

The likes and dislikes expressed about Kauai by my pollees covered the spectrum. Let me give you a few examples. First the *likes.*

"Guests from Mainland to share the beauty of our island. River view, quiet" (Wailua Homesteads, Kapaa).

"Beautiful view of both the ocean and the mountains. Because of constant breezes, never hot" (Bruce Adams, whose beautiful home in Koloa I've been privileged to visit).

"This is a quiet country island where people are still neighbors" (Lihue).

"Peaceful place to live. Close to mountains, beach, and shopping area" (Kapaa).

"The view of the mountains and the sea" (Kapaa).

"I like the tradewinds and the people. It's not like living in a big city" (Kealia).

"Quiet. Good neighbors" (Lihue).

"Town convenience and country location" (Huleia, just outside of Lihue—not on most maps).

"Slow pace of our island."

"Uncluttered, no parking meters, no need for artificial heat" (Lihue).

"No overcrowding on Kauai. Beauty of the land and coast" (Lihue).

"The wonderful people of Kauai."

And now the *dislikes* (omitting the omnipresent "high cost of living").

"Nothing" (several pollees said this).

"Possibility that this island will become like Honolulu."

"Breezes tend to be too strong—must average 20 to 30 m.p.h. most of year" (on the coast near Koloa).

"Expense of travelling off the island" ($19 one-way to Honolulu).

"Mosquitoes."

"Constant wind" (Koloa again).

"Taxes."

"My neighbor."

"Provinciality."

WRAP-UP

Bruce Adams, whom I've mentioned before, asked me to pass this advice along: "Remember if you plan to live on Kauai that the Japanese are the majority and mixtures are the rule, and you (as a *haole*) will be the minority. If you can adjust to this idea and not try to change everyone to your way of thinking and living, you'll get along just fine."

Mrs. Von Stroheim, also mentioned before, offers the following advice: "The most important words to leave on the Mainland are 'Where I come from we do it like. . . .' The most important thing to know is that Kauai is all minority groups. You must be willing to learn how to live as a minority or else don't bother to come. The day of The Great White Father complex is almost over, thank God!"

And from young Jeannie Boaz, who was my waitress one evening at Reuben's, came these words: "I have lived here in a plantation shack, a van, a tree house, a tent, and am now renting a one room house near the foot of the mountains. Life here is filled with beauty and peace. The only problems one has are self-created. With each different part of the island, experiences are many, each new and interesting. People change greatly in some ways when they have lived here any length of time.

"I only hope Kauai will remain a peaceful island full of love for nature. But with progress and tourists who don't appreciate the magic of Kauai I can see Kauai, Maui, and the other islands turning into another Oahu. It is a shame.

"Come only if you can relax and enjoy the slowness and

natural beauty. If you're looking for a fast pace, stay where you are. Come if you can appreciate and love.''

Kauai's attractions are many: lovely beaches, spectacular scenery, varied recreational facilities (especially for hikers and campers), lack of congestion. There's plenty of room to expand for industry, housing, and agriculture.

For a new resident from a Mainland city, dissatisfaction might come from the small-town atmosphere. Outside of Lihue only villages are found—and Lihue is so small that if you move around you'll keep seeing the same people every day. If you *like* a small-town environment—many folks do—this might be the place for you.

Jobs are scarce, retail opportunities limited, industrial opportunities excellent for those with capital looking for long-haul economic development.

For serious-minded young people, Kauai rates high in my book. Which reminds me of another young waitress who, in answer to my question as to why she chose Kauai over other islands, responded "This is where I went broke." Kauai is not a good place to go broke, but for intelligent, industrious people with a job, it is a good place to keep from going broke and to enjoy living while working.

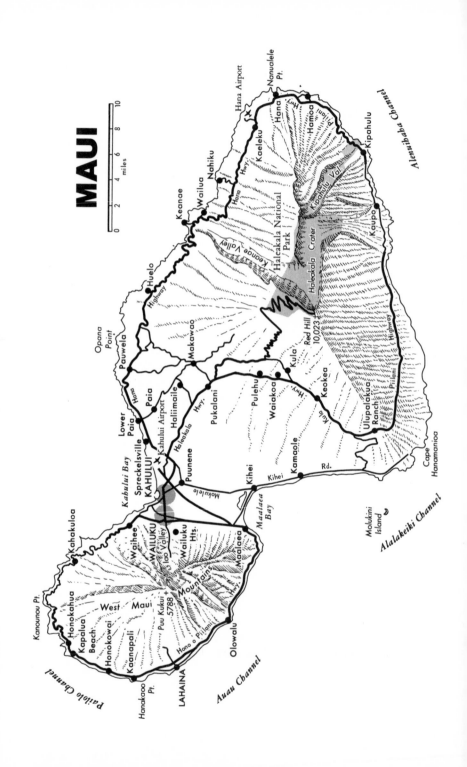

MAUI

miles
0 2 4 6 8 10

Nanualele Pt.

Alenuihaha Channel

Hana Airport

Hana Hwy.

Hamoa

Kaeleku

Hana

Kipahulu

Nahiku

Wailua

Kaupo

Keanae

Koolau Vol.

Haleakala National Park

Haleakala Crater

Huelo

Keanae Valley

Highway

Opana Point

Makawao

Red Hill 10,023

Pauwela

Hana

Paia

Pukalani

Pulehu

Kula

Piilani Hwy.

Lower Paia

Haliimaile

Waiakoa

Keokea

Kula Hwy.

Kahului Airport

Spreckelsville

KAHULUI

Puunene

Haleakala Hwy.

Kamaole

Ulupalakua Ranch

Kabului Bay

Mokulele

Kihei

Kihei Rd.

Cape Hanamanioa

Kahakuloa

Waihee

WAILUKU

Iao Valley

Wailuku Hts.

Maalaea

Maalaea Bay

Molokini Island

Alalakeiki Channel

Kanounou Pt.

Honokahua

Kapalua

Honokowai

West Maui

Puu Kukui +5788

Mountains

Olowalu

Auau Channel

Beach

Kaanapali

Hono o Piilani

Paeiolo Channel

Hanakaoo Pt.

LAHAINA

17

Maui: The Valley Island

Maui makes one wonder why there is so much
beauty so distant from so many people.—Mrs.
Marie Anderson, formerly of St. Joseph, Missouri,
now living on Oahu.

Yes, Maui has beauty. Maui has tranquility. Maui also has
progress. Put them all together, and there is sound basis for the
long-time boast of Maui's people—and others: *Maui no ka oi*,
meaning Maui is the best.

Whenever I look at a map of Maui (MOW-ee), I see it as the
body and head of a Mauian bent in supplication, asking that
Maui not be overwhelmed by progress and people. So far the
prayers have been answered. Progress has been pleasantly
moderate, and people number around 45,000.

Maui is second only to the Big Island in size. Once it was two
islands—two volcanoes: Puu Kukui and Haleakala. Eruptions
of the former built the verdant cane-filled valley lying between
them and provided the nickname "Valley Island." Haleakala,
rising to more than 10,000 feet, towers over Maui and is the
world's largest dormant volcano, with a crater 21 miles in
circumference.

We'll start our tour of Maui at the airport, on the edge of
Maui's second largest and fastest-growing town, Kahului (population 9,000). We'll do the most scenic route first, driving east
along the coast (along the back of my bowing Mauian) as far as
the historic Seven Pools.

The highway (No. 36) passes through sugar-cane fields, bypassing the fine residential community of Spreckelsville and the
fairways of the low-key Maui Country Club, which has a 9-hole
golf course open to the public and excellent dining facilities for
members only.

On the left comes Baldwin Park, which offers picnicking and camping facilities. The beach is not the finest on the island for swimming, but is adequate. This is the windward side of Maui, and the breezes are sometimes too strong to be pleasant. Adjoining the park is a Buddhist mission with mausoleums that resemble small oriental houses.

At the village of Paia just beyond, we'll see old nondescript store buildings and a Buddhist temple with a giant gong, which sounds each morning and night.

Past Paia we're really in rural Maui, and our concentration now will be on nature: beaches, waterfalls, and spectacular scenery. Across the pineapple fields on our right loom massive Haleakala and its cloud blanket.

Kaumahina State Park atop a cliff immediately on the right is worth a stop for the view below. Most first-timers make side trips to the villages of Keanae and Wailua, almost unbelievably picturesque.

Next stop is one of my favorite spots in Hawaii, tiny Puaa Kaa State Park with two bathing pools, each fed by a waterfall. Last time Melva and I stopped here, someone had left an empty Colonel Sanders Fried Chicken box under the lone picnic table. It flawed an otherwise perfect scene. And with a rubbish container close at hand!

After the Hana Airport comes Wainapanapa State Park with low-rental cottages. Then Hana Bay and the village of Hana. This area is largely owned by the Hana Ranch, which operates an informal, de luxe hotel, the Hana Maui (formerly the Hana Ranch Hotel), and a shopping center. Right on the highway is the Hasegawa General Store, which sells most everything, including bumper stickers reading "Fight Smog—Buy Horses."

Beyond, the road leads to Seven Pools, center of a conservationist battle some years ago. Now the area is incorporated in the Haleakala National Park. The pavement ends shortly beyond the pools. One could continue on a scenic loop around to meet Highway 37 at the southwest corner of Maui, but I haven't met anyone who advises it.

The seven pools formed by the cascading waters seeking the sea afford an outstanding place to frolic in the water. You can picnic on the rocks near the water, but Melva and I prefer the grassy knoll higher up under the pandanus trees.

From where we began our tour, we could have driven southeast instead on Route 37 through cane-crowded uplands, and ranchlands to the wooded area called Kula, which at elevations around 4,000 feet attracts visitors and residents who prefer fireplace evenings to the tropical warmth of the seaside.

After Kula the road climbs crookedly to Haleakala National Park. Park headquarters are at 7,000 feet. Your first view of the crater comes at Kalahaku Overlook (9,300 feet). Then comes the Visitor Center (only 36 miles from the sea-level airport) at 9,700 feet. The observatory, a bit farther up the road at more than 10,000 feet, affords an exciting 360° view. It can be a lonely spot. At 1 P.M. on July 31, 1971, for example, Melva and I were the only persons there—the only spot in the world that can be reached by road in 40 miles from sea level to 10,000 feet.

I won't go into detail about the crater, but a quote from Mark Twain might be in order. After ascending by horse and spending a chilly night around a fire, he viewed the sunrise over the crater and described it as "the sublimest spectacle I ever witnessed and I think the memory of it will remain with me always." I'll take Mark's word for it. B-r-r-r-!

I won't tell you how Haleakala, which means House of the Sun, got its name. It's a story that any Maui school child can relate more entertainingly than I.

From the airport we could have proceeded (via Routes 38, 35, and 31) almost due south to the end of the pavement shortly before Makena Beach. We would have passed through vast canefields before reaching the coast at Kihei. The coast is lined with beaches, beach parks, residences, one big hotel (the Maui Lu), and numerous apartments and apartment-hotels. Swimming is good at many spots. Kamaole County Park is perhaps the favorite place to swim, judging by the crowds I have seen there on Sundays—but not during the week. To the east the land sloping upward toward Haleakala is developing as subdivisions. At Makena plans long afoot for a gigantic development are materializing. The new Wailea Golf Course will soon be surrounded by hotels and condominiums.

Our final jaunt will be around the "head" of my mythical Mauian. From the airport we will drive west through the twin towns of Kahului and Wailuku on Route 36, switching at the far end of Wailuku to Route 30.

Just before Kahului you'll see a pond on the right, which is a sanctuary for the rare Hawaiian stilt, a bird that once was approaching extinction.

As we enter Kahului, we'll see on the left a new shopping center, the Maui Mall. Beyond it is an older one, the Kahalui Shopping Center, and then comes another new one, the Kaahumanu Center. I have spent several pleasant hours at the Kahalui center sitting on a bench under the monkeypod trees and listening to the old men who gather to reminisce and to play cards.

Just past the shopping centers on the other side of the road is a string of tourist hotels: the Maui Hukilau, the Maui Palms, and the Maui Beach, all on the shore of Kahului Harbor, Maui's commercial port. Then comes one of the larger foodstores on the island, Foodland, a branch of the island-wide chain.

On the left a residential district of comfortable middle-class houses stretches up the slopes. On the right comes Maui Community College, then sport facilities, and the Baldwin High School.

Kahului and Wailuku share a common boundary that zigzags across here. On the left of the road and up a hill is the Maui Memorial Hospital. On the right on the bluffs are residences with a fine view of the harbor.

Crossing a highway overpass brings us to the older portion of Wailuku's Main Street. This street and the intersecting Market Street a few blocks ahead constitute the heart of Wailuku's downtown section, which even the Chamber of Commerce admits is decadent. Plans have long been afoot for rehabilitating this area and other parts of historic Wailuku, but at this writing I've seen nothing concrete (pun intended).

Beyond the Market Street intersection are a few modern buildings, notably the eight-story Wailuku Townhouse (condominium apartments, in one of which my wife and I lived while working on this book—and fine living it was). Next door is a six-story medical building, and across the street the State Office Building, which I find aesthetically pleasing.

Turning left at the State Office Building, we see a wooden church built in 1837. Its backdrop is the historic Iao Valley and Puu Kukui volcano. If we had proceeded straight up the hill instead of turning left, we would see on the left the Maui Historical Society Museum, as we began the three-mile climb to a dead-end at the Iao Valley State Park for a view of the Iao Needle, a promontory rising sharply to an elevation of 2,250 feet. It is often veiled in clouds. On the left en route is Heritage Park, a favorite picnic spot for local people. When finished, it will include Chinese, Japanese, Filipino, Portuguese, Hawaiian, and early American gardens.

Now back at that church. Across the street is the modern post office and the County Police Department. On the right is the Wailuku Library, and on the left the new nine-story County Office Building. On the mountainside on the right is Wailuku Heights, a favored residential district.

Soon we leave Wailuku behind and drive south through the inevitable canefields to Maalaea Bay. (A short detour here would bring us to a pleasant little boat harbor.) Highway 30 bends to the right at the bay and follows the coast along tree-shaded beaches, some with black sand.

The first destination of interest, other than the beaches, is the old whaling town of Lahaina, only lightly touched by the hand of today's architects. Most of the homes are old and garden-clad. The main street, called Front Street, is a curiosity-rousing mixture of old and pseudo-old buildings and tourist-oriented shops.

A walking tour is outlined in a brochure available from the Hawaii Visitors Bureau. My wife and I did the tour one rainy Sunday afternoon and enjoyed a wet traipse through the ancient cemeteries, the old stone prison, and a dry return to the friendly corner bar of the Pioneer Inn on the waterfront. This inn was built in 1901 but gives the illusion of much greater age. The inn and its environs are the tourist heart of Lahaina. Here charter boats (fishing and glass-bottomed varieties) await customers; here outdoor dining and pleasant shopping attract residents and tourists. Next door to the inn on the south is the old courthouse, now housing a cooperative art gallery in the basement and police headquarters upstairs. Nearby is what is billed as the largest banyan tree in Hawaii. Across from the tree, on Front Street, is an al fresco restaurant appropriately named The Banyan Inn, the historic Baldwin House, The Whale's Tale (another first-class restaurant), and miscellaneous shops.

Proceeding down Front Street, we pass shop after shop in the first block. Then, on the left, is a seawall with benches and the ocean just beyond. Shops and restaurants continue on the right side and soon appear again on the left. I'll have more to say about Lahaina shops later.

Some of the finest beaches in Hawaii lie north of Lahaina. The first long stretch, known as Kaanapali, has been taken over by a resort complex of luxury hotels and condominiums built around the fairways of two expensive golf courses. There is a fancy shopping center here called Whaler's Village, complete with the skeleton of a 40-foot sperm whale and other objects related to whaling on display. A modern innovation, the likes of which never existed in the whaling days, is the Lahaina-Kaanapali and Pacific Railroad. It carries tourists between a station in Kaanapali and the north edge of Lahaina. For an extra fare, tandem buses somewhat resembling old-time streetcars scurry among the hotels, picking up and delivering vacation-commuters.

North of Kaanapali the shoreline becomes more pleasing, with a series of bays and variations in elevation. Here are located many small hotels and condominium apartments. Some of the condominiums are in fact investment properties for short-term rentals, but designed and sold as condominiums to circumvent the more stringent building restrictions applicable to hotels.

The northernmost developments are in the Napili area. Kapalua (Fleming) Beach here is Melva's favorite, especially at sunset. North and east of Napili the mountainous land is mostly inhabited by grazing cattle and horses.

The scenery is magnificent as the road rises and falls, winding tortuously around the top of the "head" of Maui all the way back to Wailuku. At the village of Waihee near Wailuku, a left turn at the ball park leads to the municipal golf course by the sea. My speedometer showed 20 miles of the road between Napili and Waihee as unpaved, but it is all traversable by car, though narrow and poorly maintained in spots. This is one of Hawaii's most scenic roads. Don't let its surface deter you from driving it.

THE A TO Z OF THE VALLEY ISLAND

Agriculture. Maui boasts of the largest cane sugar plantation in the United States. Its 30,000 acres are the property of the Hawaiian Commercial and Sugar Company, whose mill is near Kahului. You've no doubt seen the C & H label on packages of sugar. This is where it comes from. The Pioneer Mill Company, with a mill near Lahaina, and the Wailuku Sugar Company are also growers of Maui's largest crop.

The other major crop was pineapple, which is being phased out. Diversified crops are grown on truck farms, affording tasty supplements to imported fruits and vegetables. Maui is famed for its onions, cabbage, and tomatoes.

Art. There are artists all over Maui. To find their work, you'd best look in Lahaina and its environs. The Lahaina Art Society is the focal point for local artists. It operates a gallery in Lahaina's historic courthouse on the harbor and sponsors lectures, classes, outdoor shows, and so forth. Sometimes, its exhibits are under THE banyan tree. There are at least two privately owned galleries in Lahaina and two in Whaler's Village, Kaanapali.

Beaches. I've covered this subject pretty well already. For more details, the Department of Parks and Recreation in the

County Building has a map showing all of the park and beach facilities.

Camping. Camp sites are shown on the above-mentioned map. For cabin camping, families and groups may arrange to use camps operated by the Boy Scouts and churches.

Churches. I can count some 20 denominations. See the Yellow Pages. Would you believe that one old church has hymn books more than a hundred years old—with no caretaker or lock on the church door?

Climate. As is true throughout Hawaii, variations in weather on Maui are more dependent on location than on season. I'm told that on the slopes of Haleakala more than 100 inches of rain can fall in a month, while 15 miles away as the birds fly is an area dryer than the Sahara. On Haleakala in December you can see snowmen; 45 minutes away you can see girls in bikinis.

Many residents live inland on slopes several hundred feet or more from the sea to obtain drier, cooler weather. Old-timers tell of icy windshields in Kula at about 4,000 feet.

Residents in various areas have told me why their weather is best. I believe each one until I talk to someone somewhere else.

Crime. Burglaries are common on Maui today, as are thefts of items from unattended autos. Old-timers say they can't get used to the need for locking everything up. Not long ago a locked house was a rarity.

Thieves are not so numerous as they are energetic. Fifty burglaries were solved with the arrest of one 19-year-old boy. The arrest of an 18-year-old solved another 22 unlawful entries. And so it goes, as I read the crime news of Maui. Suspended sentences follow many arrests. More crimes follow some suspended sentences. Maui was shocked, but I wasn't, by the Yuletide theft of five gift-wrapped packages from an unlocked station wagon parked at the Kahului Shopping Center.

Theft is not the worst crime that makes the news. Physical attacks, some of a sexual nature, are not uncommon. Female hitchhikers have been victims.

Non-sexual attacks by local youths on longhaired transients, while not to be condoned, become more understandable when viewed in the context of the non-conformance by many hippies with local customs in such matters as appearance, housing, willingness to work, and respect for private property. Some nice, hard-working people look like hippies and suffer accordingly.

Ecology. The motto *Maui no ka oi* is taken seriously by Mauians. Maui is the best, say they, and they are striving to keep it that way.

There are problems. Cars multiply like rabbits. High-rise hotels go up with undistinguished design or, as has been said of some, with no visible design in the artistic sense of the word. Cane fields still burn, and mills still smoke.

But Mauians are alert to pollution in all of its forms. Take, for instance, water pollution, I understand that Maui leads not only the state of Hawaii but also most comparable areas of the Mainland in dealing with water pollution problems, particularly of sewage. And take the problem of litter. Anti-litter campaigns are perhaps succeeding no better on Maui than on the other islands, but Maui may win the battle a generation from now, for it is fighting hard at the teenage and sub-teenage levels. Nowhere but on Maui have I seen garbage cans labeled, "Feed Me!"

When I called upon the County Planning Director, he gave me copies of the long-range development plans for the island. The plans are impressive. Will they be implemented? "Yes," some say. "They won't be," say others. Time will tell.

Education. More than 10,000 Maui children attend 23 public and 10 private schools. Maui Community College at Kahului and the Mauna Olu Campus of the U.S. International University at Paia offer advanced education.

Seabury Hall, at Makawao, is operated by the Episcopal Churches of Hawaii. A highly regarded day and boarding school for boys and girls of grades 7 to 12, it draws students from all over Hawaii and the Mainland.

Employment. Newcomers may have to do a lot of job-seeking and may not find what they want or the salary they would like. The state employment office can be helpful, as can private employment services. My wife once advertised in the *Maui News* for a "temporary secretarial job or what have you" and got no response, but through the employment services she had several offers of permanent positions. Finally, she landed a short-term job with an insurance agent. She considered answering the call of the pineapple cannery for extra help, but shied off when she learned it was a 10-hour day and she would have to alternate day and night shifts.

My nomination for the job of the year, although the hours are not to my taste, goes to that held by Bettie Nesheim, age 55. She delivers newspapers in Kula from 3:30 A.M. to 6 A.M. This is what Mrs. Nesheim told me about her job:

"It's hard to know where to begin to describe all the delightful things one sees at those hours—cane fires lighting up the sky—so many stars, close enough to touch it seems—a rainbow over Makawao seen by the light of the full moon in palest color, perfect! Or maybe colts playing in the pasture—romping like kittens. New baby calves, to watch grow up. Then again, people! Most delightful are my morning visits with Grandmom Gregulho at the little Kula bakery. Her always cheerful self can't help but make my day better for having stopped to chat. At past 80 this dear soul does more work in a morning than most of us would tackle in a month—and cheerfully. The aromas of fresh bread and firewood are incomparable too." (I nominate Grandmom as jobholder of the years.)

As for business opportunities, let me give you the story of Mary Adwell, founder of Jamar Health Foods, Kahului Shopping Center.

"I had long wanted to open a health food store as I am greatly concerned about the quality of food today. Never in a million years would I have dared to even consider such an undertaking anywhere but here, especially with no money. I did it before I found out it couldn't be done. The shoestring I started on was so short it is nothing short of a miracle that we now have a thriving business. With prayer, faith, and the help of former drug addicts who had become Christians the store became a reality and has been a success beyond my wildest expectations. I had so much help and good wishes it couldn't fail! I wouldn't especially recommend opening a business here for anyone else as the chances for failure are as great as for success, but it can be done."

Entertainment. Commercial entertainment centers in Lahaina and in the hotels in Kahului and Kaanapali.

But Mauians don't depend on indoor entertainment. Listen as Mrs. Lee Abrams, who describes herself as a young grandmother, tells about some of her activities:

"Recently we rode into and through Haleakala Crater to the far side where there is a lush green oasis with two cabins, ripe plums, blackberries, and a lovely corral. We watched rare nene (a goose—the Hawaiian state bird), pheasant, and herds of wild goats. Cooking was with wood, lighting by kerosene lamps.

"Two weeks before over a hundred of us sailed to Lanai for a steak fry. We slept on the beach and gathered for brunch before sailing back.

"Some great satisfactions for me have been helping to found the Lahaina Yacht Club, the Maui Horse Owners Association, the County Board of Realtors, etc."

Speaking of horses, Mrs. Wicksted, formerly of El Monte, California, told me she had never enjoyed a rodeo on the Mainland more than those held annually at Makawao on Maui. Mrs. Wicksted went on to say that she and her husband love Maui and never find a dull moment. Neither do most Mauians.

Fishing. Most deep-sea fishing is done from charter boats out of Lahaina. As far as I know, there is no fresh-water fishing on Maui, owing to the nature of the mountainous, volcanic terrain and the few natural fresh-water bodies of water.

Golf. I've played only the municipal course and the country club course, which I found were first-class, cheap, and uncrowded during the week. The Royal Kaanapali golf course sometimes offers a special distraction during the winter: humpback whales spouting offshore.

Government. Maui County (which includes the nearby islands of Molokai, Lanai, and Kahoolawe—see later listings) is governed by an elected Mayor and a nine-member Council with two-year terms.

Hiking. Hiking is big sport on Maui. Iao Needle, for instance, offers a challenge. There is no record of anyone climbing it between 1914 and 1967, but it has since been scaled in about 4 hours, round trip. A more common hiking area is the crater of Haleakala, where the cabins afford good overnight accommodations.

Hotels. In addition to many large hotels, some of which I have spoken of, Maui offers a selection of more modest hotels and apartment-hotels along its coast and in Wailuku and Kahului. Kula has two rustic inns, the Silversword Inn and Kula Lodge, at pleasant elevations.

Housing. Of the Neighbor Islands, Maui has the best housing opportunities for newcomers, it appears from my discussions with realtors and study of classified ads.

The main areas where newcomers are most likely to live are Kahului-Wailuku, Pukalani, Kula, Kihei, and Lahaina (with which I include the area to the north along the coast).

For moderate-priced housing, fast-growing Kahului (population 9,000) is a good bet, because it has many new houses and more being built. The big landholder in this area, Alexander and Baldwin, describes it as the bedroom community for much of Maui.

About 10 miles upland from Kahului is the Pukalani area, which is also growing. Developments here will add many houses during the late seventies and, so it is planned, a golf course.

Above Pukalani in the Kula area most of the homes are expensive and have acreage. It is fine for people with means who want to live at an elevation of about 4,000 feet and maybe keep some animals.

In Kihei most of the recent development has been in condominiums, some of them high-rise. This area is developing fast as a resort and residential area.

Lahaina and the coast north of it offer housing of wide variety. The Kaanapali area attracts the wealthy, especially golfers. North of Kaanapali are apartments and small tracts for sale. Realtors will give you the full picture at the drop of a hint of interest.

Hunting. Maui is highly favored by hunters. Controlled hunting may be enjoyed in the Kula Game Management Area (game birds) and in Haleakala National Park (wild goats).

Industry. Except for the manufacture of raw sugar, food processing is done only in a few small plants. Clothes, jewelry, and wood products are manufactured on a small scale.

Kahoolawe. One of the four islands that make up the County of Maui, Kahoolawe lies just off of Kihei. Inhabited only by wild animals and birds, it is off-limits to humans, because the military forces have long used it as a bombing target.

Lanai. The island of Lanai, part of the County of Maui, is almost totally owned by the Dole Corporation. Not surprisingly, it has the world's largest pineapple plantation—at season's height more than a million pineapples are shipped out daily. It also has a fine beach (Manele), more Norfolk pines than palms, a free 9-hole golf course, about 20 miles of paved roads, and a well-run modest hotel, Lanai Lodge, where Melva and I recently spent a pleasant weekend. Lanai is a fine place to swim, hunt, fish, golf, or relax. Development plans are in the offing. Right now, except for employees of Dole, there isn't much opportunity for new residents.

Libraries. The public libraries in Kahului and Wailuku are adequate to meet most needs, as are the smaller ones in Lahaina and Makawao. (The personnel of all of them were helpful in the preparation of this book.) Film programs for children and adults are frequently scheduled. A bookmobile tours the island.

Maui Potato Chips. The Kobayashi family has for 20 years or so produced limited quantities of incomparable potato chips. The trade name is *Kitch'n Cook'd,* but they're known simply as Maui potato chips. They have been described as dark, heavy, brittle, gnarled chunks of fried potato.

Medical Facilities. The modern Maui Memorial Hospital has 152 beds. The Kula Sanatorium and General Hospital has 220 beds; it cares for tubercular, mental, and long-term patients.

Military. There are no major military installations on Maui.

Molokai. The island of Molokai, part of the County of Maui, has the distinction of having a separate county within it, Kalawao County. That county (the Kalaupapa peninsula) is administered by the Department of Health, because it is occupied by the state's century-old leprosy isolation center, made famous by Father Damien. Now that the disease is less feared, it has been proposed that the area be incorporated into Maui County and a cable constructed to relieve its dependence upon boats, planes, or hikers for contact with the rest of Molokai. Molokai is largely devoted to the cultivation of pineapples, but they are being phased out. It affords fine golfing, hunting, and fishing. It offers excellent accommodations in the Hotel Molokai and the Pau Hana Inn. Housing is so scarce, despite a few new apartments, that no casual newcomer should, in my opinion, consider Molokai as a residence at this time. Development plans come and go, but at least one, that of the Kaluakoi Corporation, has reached the action stage.

Museums. The Maui Historical Society Museum occupies the Wailuku home, built in 1841, of missionary Edward Bailey, grandfather of Edward Wilson, Jr., the affable young district manager of the Hawaii Visitors Bureau. Displays dating back to the pre-Captain Cook era include outstanding furniture and household items of the missionary period. I'm sure you would enjoy, as my wife and I have, the annual garden parties held on the grounds in July.

Worth a visit in Lahaina is the Baldwin House, the oldest building on Maui, now open as a museum with a worthy collection of memorabilia of missionary days.

Newspapers. The *Maui News* is published three times a week with a weekly supplement, *Holiday in Maui,* which is tourist-oriented but useful to residents as well. *The Maui Sun* is a lively weekly tabloid.

Radio and Television. Maui has two radio stations and relays of Oahu television stations. On the Lahaina side, cable television brings television channels and FM radio stations.

Restaurants. Considering that tourists tend to eat in their hotels and residents at home, Maui has a surprising number of attractive restaurants. Here's a rundown by area of some favored by local residents. The list is not complete, even though I have excluded the hotels, most of which serve fine meals.

	Wailuku–Kahului
The Landing	Businessmen's favorite.
	Harbor setting.
	Makawao
Club Rodeo Steak House	Prime rib dinner Monday
	and Thursday nights, $5.
	Kula
Kula Lodge	Rustic ambience.
Silversword	Circular fireplace in the
	middle.
	Lahaina
Banyan Inn	Very popular.
Chez Paul	Excellent French food.
Whale's Tale	Top chefs.

Let me add a few specialty places that newcomers might otherwise overlook, to their disadvantage.

Aloha Restaurant	Hawaiian food. Kahului.
Gate 21	Try the Portuguese soup.
	Airport.
Golden Palace	Good Chinese cuisine.
	Lahaina Shopping Center.
Kurasaki Cafe	Tiny, Japanese. Kahului.
Mama's Fish House	On the beach at Kuau.
Tree Garden	Three levels. Imaginative
	menu. Lahaina Market Place.

Senior Citizens. I am acquainted with many retirees from the Mainland on Maui. Some are living in luxury on the edge of golf courses in modern condominiums. Others are living simply in the Kula uplands, growing most of their own food. I find them almost universally happy.

Shopping. Looking back, I see that I have mentioned all of the major shopping centers except the Whaler's Village in Kaanapali. It is nicely designed—a combination museum and shopping center. Its 30 or so shops (they always seem to be adding more) include a branch of Liberty House.

Some residents used to complain that Maui's stores were geared to low-income people. That is no longer true.

Now then let's talk about food. The cost of my market basket of groceries was about the same in the two stores I shopped in, one in Kahului and one in Lahaina; the average was 7 percent more than the Oahu average.

I mentioned earlier that Maui is famed for its onions. One man even told me that he moved to Maui for the potato chips and Kula onions. An agriculture official told my wife that the Kula onion is a Texas hybrid. He said that the Texas onion is hotter because they season it in the sun, drying it out and giving it a sharper taste. The Kula onion, on the other hand, is juicy. Juice spurts when you cut one. Did you ever see a portrait of an onion? Jim Warren, once a Hollywood actor, paints Kula onion portraits—and what is more, he sells them for more than $50 each. He eats them, too. So do we—batter-fried.

On Maui onions are eulogized in oils, and a store is eulogized in song. Hasegawa's General Store is also a popular song by the same name. Don't ask the local disk jockeys to play it though. I once heard one of them tell a caller that he'd play it if Mr. Hasegawa would send in $10 for the commercial. I'll end this food talk on a savory note by telling you that if you grew up eating catfish, as I did in Missouri, you won't have to forgo them in Hawaii if the catfish hatchery—prawns too—of Fish Farms continues its initial success.

Tennis. The county maintains free tennis courts at five or more localities. Some of the de luxe hotels have courts, as does the Racquet Club Condominiums. The Royal Lahaina Tennis Ranch has six courts—enough for professional tennis tournaments.

Tourism. Tourism is a carefully nurtured industry on Maui, despite the opposition of those who consider it a blight. Given the large number of hotel rooms available, it would be a serious blow to the economy if tourism declined. On the other hand, I side with my conservation-minded friends in wishing that Maui would not build many more hotel rooms and pseudo-con-dominium apartments to serve as hotels.

Transportation. Maui has the finest network of highways of all Hawaii, and they're uncrowded. Additional arteries in the valley—the heartland—can be cut through the canefields with comparative ease and low cost, as needed, to serve the growing population and tourist industry.

The only public transportation on the island (other than the tourist train) that I know of is a bus line between Lahaina and the Napili area and a shuttle service between the airport and Kaanapali.

Barge service carries inter-island cars and freight.

The inter-island airlines are supplemented by charter service. Ask the Hawaii Visitors Bureau for details of air services, which are subject to frequent operational and fare changes.

Youth. Maui has long been a hippie haven. A brochure for the guidance of newcomers bears a map and description of camping facilities and points out that hitchhiking is prohibited, camping in county parks is by permit only, public nudity is prohibited, and so on.

But the Mauian approach to the transient invasion is not all negative. The county operates with some success a juvenile counseling service for first offenders and those who are in danger of becoming delinquent. Businessmen and transients have cooperated in cleanup programs. The Teen Challenge center has been a godsend for youths with drug problems.

The youth program with which I am most familiar is one in which my wife has participated. Here's what Richard Winkler, Rector of the Church of the Good Shepherd, told me about it:

"The Church of the Good Shepherd on selected evenings operates a coffee house known as The Turning Point. The average attendance is about 60. Good entertainment is provided. This is a Christian coffee house, attracting all races and ages and life styles. A number of 'Jesus People' are in attendance, as well as locals, and adults. Coffee and tea and popcorn, sometimes cakes, are provided free, and a soft drink machine is available. This has been a place where all types can get together on a common basis and 'rap' and just plain enjoy themselves. The operation of the coffee house is by the young people, with adult supervision. Entertainment is by people of all ages, sometimes as young as 8 or 9 years old. We have much good guitar playing, modern religious folk and gospel singing, Christian witnessing, etc. but no pressure is put on anyone. Here young people can come together and have fun and fellowship with like-minded youth."

Z. Zero is what I've batted trying to zero in on a zippy closer, despite my zeal in zeeking one. So by zooks and zounds I'll close this zection like a zipper. Zoom!

WHAT RESIDENTS LIKE AND DISLIKE ABOUT MAUI

The *likes* and *dislikes* of Mauians follow pretty much the same pattern as those on the other Neighbor Islands, so let's skip the details. I'll give you just a few striking comments of pollees.

"I have never felt freer and more surrounded by kindness and love."

"I like it because my cost of living is less than it was in Seattle and living here is so much more fun."

"To me Maui seems like a small world. Instead of seeing only a small part of the world, here I get the feeling I can grasp it all."

"I like seeing both ends of a rainbow in one scenic panorama. Watching the sunrise from Haleakala and the lei of clouds that often forms around the mountain. The smell of white ginger and plumeria. The beauty of a single bloom of night blooming cereus."

The only dislike I'm going to mention here is that of Gordon Gibson, the genial Canadian owner of the Maui Lu Resort in Kihei. My wife and I met Mr. Gibson when we rented one of the seaside cottages of his resort, which is outstanding, particularly for family groups. A man in his upper sixties, he impressed us with his vitality. It seemed that everywhere I looked I saw Mr. Gibson working at something from dawn to dusk, even watering plants and flowers. Mr. Gibson (who since that time has been married) told me that the only thing he dislikes about Maui is the thought of dying.

WRAP-UP

My prose is less adequate than the words of politicians to describe Maui. Listen to this:

"The grandeur and the tranquility of Maui's Haleakala has always been an influence upon my inner spirit. Born in Maui, I am a child of its seashore, its tropical jungles, its streams and valleys. Nature's extravagance is resplendent on Maui. May we always want to return there" (Patsy T. Mink, Member of Congress).

And this:

"While much of Hawaii has become one of the most famous resorts in the world, Maui, developing intelligently, has remained the Hawaii spoken of in song and legend. Untarnished by clusters of high-rise hotels and smog-producing freeways, Maui offers the visitor and resident a way of life unquestionably unique in the world" (Elmer F. Cravalho, Mayor).

Some say that it takes a bit of time to get adjusted to life on Maui. Here are two illustrative comments on the subject.

"Be sure you can take island living, and try it out for a while before burning all the bridges. If the move has been made, stick it out for a while before going back. It takes a few months to get over the cultural shock and the insular feeling, but after that there is *no place like Hawaii (and Maui)*" (clergyman).

"A friend of mine hated it here and couldn't wait to get away, but it was only about three weeks before she was writing me that she couldn't wait to get back. She made it about a month ago and is very happy here. As she says, 'Maui does something to you!' "

Lest you get too carried away by those words of praise for Maui, let me add some precautionary advice from a smart woman I quoted earlier in the chapter:

"Anyone thinking of moving here should come with an open mind. Want to get to know the people and love them. Not have pre-conceived prejudices. Have patience. Learn to live by and enjoy Hawaiian time. Accept pidgin as part of the culture. Enjoy!" (Bettie Nesheim, newsgirl).

THE DECISION TO MOVE TO HAWAII

18
Making the Decision

Make sure you can adjust to island living and that
you understand the housing and cost of living situation, particularly if you have a large family.—
Stephen N. White, formerly of La Jolla, California.

Some come to Hawaii only for a temporary or seasonal sojourn
—which takes only mood and money. Others come because
they have little or no choice: military personnel under orders
and businessmen who get sent by their company.

This chapter is not written primarily for those people, but for
readers contemplating a permanent or indefinite period of residence by choice: job-seekers, independent businessmen, and
coupon-clippers. For them, serious decision-making is in order.

Hawaii is not for everyone. Some like it from the start. Others
don't. Dorothy Read, once a secretary in California, now a
Honolulu housewife, put it nicely when she told me, "Living in
Hawaii is like falling in love—it happens to some of us but not to
all. Once you're struck by a love of Hawaii you're hooked—
you'll want to stay. But it doesn't happen to all."

But Mrs. Read isn't completely correct. Some are enthusiastic at first but become disenchanted after a bit. Take a look at
these excerpts from a letter written to my wife by an acquaint-
ance, who was about to leave Hawaii with her husband to move
to New Mexico after three years of residence here:

"Anyone moving to Hawaii should bring money, and lots of
it, or be prepared for a much lower standard of living than they
have ever cared to think about. The price differential is stag-
gering. If they do not mind paying outrageous rent for a shack in
which they might be ashamed to entertain, they will be in great
shape.

"I think the people who live out their days in Hawaii happily,
may be divided into two major categories. Either they have very

narrow interests and horizons, and/or perhaps dislike travelling altogether, or else have a multitude of financial resources and can travel at will. Most of us here cannot even afford a trip to the outer islands, unless it is for a once-a-year vacation. Many people in Honolulu only venture to the leeward or windward sides of Oahu every year or so.

"As for education, the best available remains in the private schools and will continue to do so as long as professors, teachers, and legislators will send their offspring to them. Those who have the power to bring about a change are little concerned because their own youngsters are at Punahou. A child who is ambitious can obtain a good education anywhere, of course, but there are problems and not all of them in the classroom, by a long shot.

"I am tempted to suggest that perhaps your book should not be written at all. However, remembering our difficulty in obtaining information about living in Hawaii, it is apparent that you would be doing a service for those who are determined to make the move.

"One final point. I would like to stress that the 'easy pace' and the 'aloha spirit' are pretty much reserved for visitors. The would-be permanent resident may find it an entirely different story."

Before press time we received another letter from this "gypsy" saying that she and her husband "are so glad to be back home!" Yes, the letter was postmarked Hawaii. We got together for lunch and I learned that they are very happy and have no plans to leave again.

Nevertheless, her first letter emphasizes the need for caution. I can assure you that Hawaii is not faced with dissident residents to the extent that California is—a survey indicated that almost a third of California's urban residents would prefer to leave.

I asked my pollees what advice, comments, or information they would like to see passed along to persons who plan to live in Hawaii. In reply, many cautioned against making an irrevocable or difficult-to-revoke move to Hawaii without a trial visit as a *householder*. Let's look at some responses.

"Come first for a few months without selling out on the Mainland because after the glitter wears off, you may *hate* it." (He's been here since 1957.)

"If a person likes all kinds of people and is willing to adapt to local conditions, Hawaii is a wonderful place. If he has prejudices in people, food, or customs he had better stay away." (She's been here since 1947.)

"Be prepared to pay more for hired help, food, and construction materials. Requires patience and time to get most items— much shopping around."

"BRING LOTS OF MONEY!" (a common comment).

"If planning to work, have a secure promise before coming. Be careful in buying property."

"Be sure to have assurance of good income. Hawaii isn't much fun if you can't really afford it."

"Jobs are hard to get unless you are 'in' here, particularly in trained fields. Come with money or an idea. Don't expect help. They hope you won't stay." (He's stayed since 1968 and is doing very well.)

"Those who need to have employment to live should come over and spend at least a month looking around and checking on climate, cost of living, way of life, wage rates, etc. It doesn't suit everybody."

"You should understand that Hawaii was once an independent country and *culturally* would still like to be free of the Mainland."

"Hawaii is not the tropical paradise that it is made out to be. Basically Honolulu is just like any other large city on the Mainland—with all their problems. On the outer islands are typical Mainland small towns." (I can't agree that these places typify the Mainland.)

"We find it is a perfect haven for people who have seen the world and want to live a quiet life" (Ingrid Elsner, in her forties).

"Come if you don't expect to find everything at the stores and can enjoy the great beauty of these islands and help them to grow well."

"Don't try to do it on a shoe string! Have plenty of money to fall back on for emergencies as well as current expenses. Transients who try to make it by 'bumming' or living the so-called hippie style are definitely not welcomed or appreciated.''

"It takes a long time for a Mainlander to get used to 'Hawaiian Time,' the slower pace, the lack of spare parts, delays in obtaining items out of stock, slowness of repairs.''

"The drug problem is acute here, too, so if anyone thinks he can escape it by moving to Hawaii, forget the move.''

"Any person who has experienced any allergy problems or asthma should spend some time here before making a definite move.''

"Have enough money to last a year to get a place to live and a suitable job.'' (Dorothy Gunn came here in 1965 and manages a dress shop.)

"Don't come to Hawaii with prejudices against others of different skin color. The aloha spirit is a state of mind. Peace must be internal as well as external.''

"Friendliness, kindness, and understanding, and accepting the way of life of those you share Hawaii with are truly essential to all interested in this Paradise'' (Mabel Wheeler, who came here from Des Moines in 1959).

"Don't move over here believing it is a Paradise. Be prepared for problems.''

"My wife and I enjoy Hawaii as it is. We are most distressed that Mainlanders move in and try to change the islands to their little town back home. It is our feeling that such people would be much happier if they had remained there.''

"I feel that Hawaii is a unique place to live. There is such a variety of people who all blend in so well with one another.''

"Don't come if you're thin-skinned about racial discrimination—there'll be some against you.''

"You'd better come several times and stay and drive all around the island you plan to live on'' (Annette McWilliams, retired teacher from Phoenix).

"Young people should be sure to find out about the hiking and 'just living on the beaches.' It's not as easy as it sounds. There are laws and limits. Many young people read items that make it seem very easy to come and live off the land—then they get here and find that they can't: no jobs, no homes, and it gets very rough on them'' (and on the taxpayers too).

''You must realize it is confined living on an island and to enjoy it you must like people of different races and customs.'' (Hector Baxter, who has lived the world over. We first met in India in the mid-fifties and see one another frequently).

I have quoted pollees at such length, not with the intention of discouraging you about a move to Hawaii, but to alert you to the disappointments that might follow a hasty or unwise decision.

I'll conclude by pointing out that an anti-newcomer feeling has surfaced in Hawaii, as it has in Florida, owing to environmental pressures and aversion to some of the newer residents. That feeling exists not only among residents native to Hawaii but also among ex-Mainlanders as well. Here's what some of them say:

''Up to three years ago I would have advised coming here if serenity and beauty unlimited come first. Now there are too many here and coming'' (More than 20 years of residence has made him proprietary).

''Stay away—there are too many of us interlopers now! (a recent interloper from California).

''Stay home. It's getting too crowded with Mainlanders now. Soon the charm that makes Hawaii what it is will wilt under yankee aggressiveness.'' (She came from Maryland in 1965.)

''I feel very strongly that Hawaii as it exists today will be ruined if more residents arrive. Newcomers go home!'' (She came in 1964.)

''The influx of Mainlanders (this does not mean tourists) must stop. I would gladly join an action group and give money to an organization willing to hire a good Mainland PR firm to spread the news on the Mainland of all the short-comings this State has to offer its permanent residents.'' (No PR firm is needed; it's all in this book.)

The comments above prompt me to suggest to prospective new residents of Hawaii that they ask themselves not only ''What can Hawaii do for me?'' but also ''What would I do for Hawaii?'' Good, I hope.

Tips for Newcomers

Be friendly to all people. Take an active part in community projects. Don't try to change these people to your ways—you are guests in their islands. Try to understand them and their way of life.— William Vandergrift, formerly of Forest Hill, California.

The quotation above puts it well. Here are some other representative suggestions from my pollees for newcomers.

"Hawaii, with its various ethnic groups may give the newcomer a feeling that he is at a disadvantage in dealing with them. Perhaps they feel the same way. The newcomer should find it interesting in meeting and dealing with the various races to find out how they think, the little courtesies they observe, their reaction to instructions, etc. For instance one might try to tell a maid how to do a better job. No matter how well phrased, she is apt to tell her friends that she was 'bawled out.' So just the art of guiding the 'local' into the desired work routine often requires considerable finesse to avoid offending. If not approached right, the worker may simply say he or she doesn't feel good and quit.

"Please accept us as we are. Don't try to compare us with Mainland people, we are not. Enjoy things as they are, the islands have a beauty all their own (Agnes Huger, who came here in 1960 from Indiana).

"Come with an open mind and a smile on your face and you will soon be infected with the aloha spirit.

"Don't get into a rut thinking you are on a small island and cannot get off to see things. At least once a month take lunch and go to a new beach; visit a different park; stop and talk to local people; ask them questions about Hawaii and how they live; invite them to your home; go to theirs. Hawaii has so many beautiful places. Stop by the roadside and drink it in and most of all *relax!*" (Dorothy Klopp, who came here in 1953).

"Don't come in like a 'know it all.' That really *bugs* us Islanders. Be willing to listen first. Don't expect service and supplies to be as readily available here as on the Mainland. Just relax and enjoy what is here. Try new foods, don't get up-tight about changes—that should be why you came here" (Bonnie Tuell).

"Be interested in people. Welcome change. Give of yourself and accept interest from others." (Mrs. Seebruck was 86 when she wrote that!)

"Get involved in community activities to insure the survival of the spirit of aloha. A lot of people must work full-time to preserve the land and culture of the Islands" (Mrs. Alfred J. Ostheimer, III, formerly of Philadelphia, who has been active in civic affairs since 1968).

"Be sure to have good legal advice on any important move. The culture here is quite different from the run-of-the-mill Mainland community."

"People who come to Hawaii should be courteous, humble, kind, clean, reverent. They should respect the desire of most to preserve the aloha spirit of generous sharing and friendly association with all races, without hauteur, criticisms, etc." (a resident since 1942).

"Be prepared for lopsided political set-up; predominance of Oriental control; pidgin-English; high cost of living—but still best in the U.S.!" (a resident since 1938).

"Watch your belongings. Buy 'No Roach.' "

"Make a concerted effort to learn the philosophy and ways of life of oriental and Hawaiian peoples."

"Don't become another one of the great aloof 'white minority.' Blend in with the people. These islanders are rich people— not in money but in character and tradition, and they're very proud."

"Come willing to fit in and do things the local way and you'll have a ball. Just leave your ideas of time behind. Also realize that each island is a small place and that news travels fast. Watch your tongue."

"Mainlanders, almost without exception, bring with them the incredible aggressive behavior of Caucasians. They know everything, have been everywhere, and in no time are experts on Hawaii and are telling everyone here how to run things. Nothing could be more damaging to their enjoyment of the islands, as they will soon run into great resistance on the part of the islanders." (She came here in 1963 from Denver.)

Now let us turn to some replies of pollees to my question "What household items, clothing, etc. would you especially advise newcomers to bring?"

"Clothing for the tropics—wash and wear cottons especially."

"Gas refrigerator to run on propane."

"Nothing except personal belongings."

"Everything you think you'll need."

"Light clothing and all furniture."

"Furniture—not much to offer in local stores."

"Electric appliances and basic furniture."

"Plenty of money and a smile."

"Summer clothing and household goods you already own. Do not buy new items to ship."

"Small items but not bulky ones as freight is quite expensive."

"Casual clothes. Cheaper to ship these and cars, too, than to buy here."

"Ship everything but heavy clothing."

"Better to buy here. There is a large variety of things appropriate for Hawaii."

"All you can load in a container, if from the West Coast."

"Sell it on the Mainland and live more simply in the islands."

"Nothing. Buy here from Sears—they service it."

"Hard goods, appliances, shoes, bedding, furniture."

"Definitely bring everything you own and sort it out here."

"All expensive cars, books, appliances."

"Sandals and shifts."

"All utensils, bedding, light clothing."

"Air conditioners if already owned."

"Any household items in good repair."

"Raincoat, sweater, walking shoes."
"All durable goods from furniture to cameras will save $ $ $ $."
"Sporting equipment."
"Essentials and heirlooms. Buy other things secondhand."
"Sell everything and start all over."
"I brought almost a whole house full and regret nothing."
"Non-metal furniture that is light, Mildew, termites, and humidity are problems."
"Bring a good small car, in new or excellent condition."
"Sleeping bag if you're going to use one."
"If we had it to do over again, we'd bring everything we had."
I also asked my pollees what they would advise newcomers *not* to bring. Here are some of the suggestions.
"Many heavy clothes." (This was common advice.)
"Furniture."
"Clothing that must be dry cleaned."
"Furs" (very common advice).
"Decide whether shipping costs outweigh cost of item here."
"Don't bring anything but money."
"Mainland shoes."
"Persian rugs."
"TV's, stereo equipment."
"Silver and brass—they will tarnish; valuable rugs—they will mildew; large cars—they are too expensive to operate."
"Due to moving expense don't bring furniture unless it is very valuable."
"Prejudices, Mainland pressures, or superior attitudes about what you did back home."
"Big car" (a common comment).
"Bulky things with sentimental attachments."
"Girdles, hose, high heeled shoes, gloves, hats." (That's the way to let yourself go, relax!)
"An untidy appearance."
"Any more indigents."
"Anything that will mildew or rust."
"Animals, because of harsh quarantine laws" (120 days at a cost of more than 200 dollars).

If you're confused by all of that conflicting advice on what to bring and not to bring, bear in mind that the advisers represent a wide variety of personalities, incomes, and living styles. At least, with that welter of advice to guide you, if you make a mistake you can blame it on what you've read here rather than on yourself; that might be some consolation.

Now I'd like to make a few suggestions that may ease your way after arrival.

1. Stop by the Hawaii Visitors Bureau, 2270 Kalakaua Avenue, in the heart of Waikiki and ask one of the helpful attendants for whatever informational material she has that might be useful to a new resident.

2. Look well before you lease or buy housing. Check the neighborhood and facilities carefully.

3. Teach your children not to put in their mouths any plants with hairy or thorny leaves, seed pods, or milky pods. Some can be lethal.

4 Hawaii sometimes has high winds and *tsunamis* (tidal waves). Respect the official warnings and you need not fear them.

5. Register *any* firearms or ammunition with the local police within 48 hours of their arrival.

6. Open a checking account in an Hawaiian bank. Checks on Mainland banks can be hard to cash. Some local banks charge for cashing other banks' checks.

7. If you're not a good swimmer and you live on Oahu, enroll in the annual "Swim to Live" program held each August under the sponsorship of the Red Cross and the *Advertiser*. Don't swim in dangerous waters.

8. If you hike, don't go alone. Be sure to leave word of your plans with some responsible person. Follow marked trails only. Don't take chances on weather, terrain, or fires.

9. Check on the motor vehicle and traffic regulations and obey them as a driver, pedestrian, or cyclist.

10. Stay out of honkytonks.

As a finale to this chapter (and this book), I am going to set down some *Do's* and *Don't's,* based upon the experience of many persons, to supplement or emphasize what you have read already in this book. I urge you to read these carefully, think about them, and abide by them. The rewards will be rich.

DO'S

1. Do your part to keep the aloha spirit alive.
2. Do make a continuing effort to learn more about Hawaii, its people, cultures, and customs.
3. Do leave behind any racial prejudices you may have.
4. Do make a continuing effort to meet and mingle with people of all backgrounds.
5. Do try to adapt your way of doing things to Hawaii's.
6. Do make it a point to visit islands other than your home base as soon as it's convenient. Go sightseeing: you'll impress your visitors later, and you'll learn a lot.
7. Do be aware of potential danger, especially for young people. Girls should not hitchhike unless they wish to invite rape.
8. Do your part to keep the aloha spirit alive. (This is worth repeating.)

DON'TS

1. Don't poke fun at things Hawaiian.
2. Don't vocally compare Hawaii and things Hawaiian with things back on the Mainland.
3. Don't avoid rubbing elbows with local foods, customs, and people.
4. Don't confine your social activities to ex-Mainlanders.
5. Don't be impatient if things don't get done as fast as you'd like.
6. Don't knock on the doors of people you've read about in this book or bombard them with letters asking questions. They didn't come to Hawaii to become tour guides in their own homes, and they probably have enough trouble keeping up with correspondence as it is—they've done their bit for you by giving information to me, a wholesaler.
7. Don't take careless potshots, or calculated ones, at the aloha spirit—you might kill Santa Claus.

To the extent that you may have found this book interesting and meaningful, thanks are due to my pollees and other contributors. Whatever errors and deficiencies it contains are mine alone, and I accept responsibility for them, unlike the author of one publication, who wrote: "If you find any mistakes, remember we try to offer something for everyone—and some people are always looking for mistakes."

Suggestions for Further Reading

Description and Travel

Bishop, Isabella Bird. *Six Months in the Sandwich Islands*. Honolulu: University of Hawaii Press, 1964. Lively letters of a traveler in an early era (1873).

Daws, Gavan. *The Illustrated Atlas of Hawaii*. Norfolk Island, Australia: Island Heritage, 1970. Modern atlas plus a miscellany of facts and features.

Gibbons, Euell. *Beachcomber's Handbook*. New York: David McKay, 1972. How to live with nature.

Goodman, Robert B. *The Hawaiians*. Norfolk Island, Australia: Island Heritage, 1970. Notable photos plus text.

Graves, William. *Hawaii*. Washington, D.C.: National Geographic Society, 1970. Colorful text and photos.

Krauss, Bob. *Here's Hawaii*. New York: Coward-McCann, 1960. A lighthearted introduction to Hawaii by Hawaii's well-known and beloved columnist.

———. *High Rise Hawaii*. New York: Coward-McCann, 1969. Mirthful essays about Hawaii after statehood.

Krell, Dorothy. *Beautiful Hawaii*. Menlo Park, Calif.: Lane Magazine and Book Company, 1972. Striking photos. Good descriptions.

University of Hawaii. *University of Hawaii Atlas*. Honolulu: University Press of Hawaii, 1973. Good reference work.

Wallace, Robert. *Hawaii*. New York: Time-Life Books, 1973. Nature study; mostly in pictures.

History and Biography

Barrow, Terence. *Incredible Hawaii*. Rutland, Vt.: Charles E. Tuttle, 1974. Oddities and facts—some as strange as fiction.

Daws, Gavan. *Shoal of Time*. New York: Macmillan, 1968. A fascinating one-volume history of the Hawaiian Islands.

Day, Arthur Grove. *Hawaii and Its People*. Rev. ed. New York: Meredith Press, 1968. Informal social and political history.

Feher, Joseph. *Hawaii: A Pictorial History*. Honolulu: Bishop Museum Press, 1969. Wonderful collection of historic photographs.

Joesting, Edward. *Hawaii: An Uncommon History*. New York: W. W. Norton, 1972. Good writing by a competent historian.

Judd, Gerrit P. *Hawaii: An Informal History*. New York: Crowell-Collier, 1961. Entertaining capsule history.

Kuykendall, Ralph S., and Day, Arthur Grove. *Hawaii: A History*. Rev. ed. Englewood Cliffs, N.J.: Prentice-Hall, 1961. Good over-all history.

Simpich, Frederick, Jr. *Anatomy of Hawaii*. New York: Coward, McCann & Geoghegan, 1971. Facts, figures, and fascinating stories.

Smith, Bradford. *Yankees in Paradise*. Philadelphia: J. B. Lippincott, 1956. The New England impact on Hawaii.

Von Tempski, Armine. *Born in Paradise*. New York: Duell, 1940. Childhood on a Maui ranch.

Natural History

Carlquist, Sherwin. *Hawaii: A Natural History*. New York: Doubleday, 1970. An authoritative account.

Cox, J. Halley. *Hawaiian Petroglyphs*. Honolulu: Bishop Museum Press, 1970. Includes maps and illustrations.

Edmondson, Charles Howard. *Hawaii's Seashore Treasures*. Hilo, Hawaii: Petroglyph Press, 1974. Sheller's delight.

Gosline, William A., and Brock, Vernon E. *Handbook of Hawaiian Fishes*. Honolulu: University of Hawaii Press, 1960. Scientific descriptions but useful to the layman.

Hawaii Audubon Society. *Hawaii's Birds*. Rev. ed. Honolulu: Hawaii Audubon Society, 1971. Descriptions and color illustrations.

Miller, Carey D., Bazore, Katherine, and Bartow, Mary L. *Fruits of Hawaii*. 4th ed. Honolulu: University of Hawaii Press, 1965. Includes nutritive values and recipes.

Munro, George C. *Birds of Hawaii*. Rev. ed. Rutland, Vt.: Charles E. Tuttle, 1960. Good descriptions and color plates.

Hosaka, Edward Yataro. *Shore Fishing in Hawaii*. Hilo, Hawaii: Petroglyph Press, 1973. Fisherman's Bible.

Neal, Marie C. *In Gardens of Hawaii*. Rev. ed. Honolulu: Bishop Museum Press, 1965. Complete guide to plants.

Stearns, Harold T. *Geology of the State of Hawaii*. 2nd ed. Palo Alto, Calif.: Pacific Books, 1977. For both professional geologists and laymen interested in earth sciences.

————. *Road Guide to Points of Geologic Interest in the Hawaiian Islands*. 2nd ed. Palo Alto, Calif.: Pacific Books, 1977. This illustrated paperback book is indispensable to anyone sightseeing in the islands.

Industries, Land, and People

Bank of Hawaii. *Annual Economic Review*. Honolulu. Yearly surveys of the economic scene.

Fuchs, Lawrence H. *Hawaii Pono*. 3rd ed. Honolulu: University of Hawaii Press, 1967. Social history.

Hawaii. Department of Planning and Economic Development. *The State of Hawaii Data Book*. Honolulu. Annual editions.

Johannessen, Edward. *The Hawaiian Labor Movement.* Boston: Bruce Humphries, 1956. A brief history.

Lind, Andrew W. *Hawaii's People.* 3rd ed. Honolulu: University of Hawaii Press, 1967. How the diverse ethnic and racial groups are becoming one people.

Language, Legend, and Culture

Buck, Peter H. *Arts and Crafts of Hawaii.* Honolulu: Bishop Museum Press, 1957. Reprinted in fourteen separate sections in 1964.

Colum, Padraic. *Legends of Hawaii.* New Haven, Conn.: Yale University Press, 1937. Fairy tales for children and adults.

Elbert, Samuel H. *Spoken Hawaiian.* Honolulu: University of Hawaii Press, 1970. Beginning textbook.

Emerson, Nathaniel B. *Unwritten Literature of Hawaii.* Rutland, Vt.: Charles E. Tuttle, 1965. All about the ancient hula.

Finney, Ben R., and Houston, James O. *Surfing: The Sport of Hawaiian Kings.* Rutland, Vt.: Charles E. Tuttle, 1966. Surfing history.

Kahananui, Dorothy M., and Anthony, Alberta P. E. *Kama'ilio Hawai'i Kakou: Let's Speak Hawaiian.* Honolulu: University of Hawaii Press, 1970. Beginning textbook.

Kelly, John M., Jr. *Folk Songs Hawaii Sings.* Rutland, Vermont: Charles E. Tuttle, 1963. A collection from Polynesia and Asia for piano and voice.

Kuck, Loraine E. *Story of the Lei.* Honolulu: Tongg Publishing Company, 1956. Illustrated. Hawaiian leis and how to make them.

Pukui, Mary Kawena, and Elbert, Samuel H. *Hawaiian Dictionary.* Honolulu: University of Hawaii Press, 1971. The definitive reference for Hawaiian vocabulary.

Art and Literature

Blanding, Don. *Hawaii Says Aloha.* New York: Dodd, Mead, 1955. Pictures and poems of Hawaii, ancient and modern.

Bushnell, O. A. *Molokai.* Cleveland: World Publishing, 1963. Novel about the leper colony.

Day, Arthur Grove, and Stroven, Carl G. *A Hawaiian Reader.* New York: Appleton-Century-Crofts, 1959. Anthology of Hawaiian literature.

———. *The Spell of Hawaii.* New York: Meredith Press, 1968. Companion volume to *A Hawaiian Reader.*

Judd, Gerrit P. *A Hawaiian Anthology.* New York: Macmillan, 1967. Literary sampler.

Lee, W. Storrs. *Hawaii: A Literary Chronicle.* New York: Funk & Wagnalls, 1967. Stories of major events.

London, Jack. *Stories of Hawaii.* New York: Appleton-Century, 1965. Entrancing tales by a gifted writer.

Loomis, Albertine. *Grapes of Canaan*. New York: Dodd, Mead, 1951. Documentary novel of the missionaries.

Michener, James A. *Hawaii*. New York: Random House, 1959. All about it.

Cookery

Bazore, Katherine. *Hawaiian and Pacific Foods*. New York: M. Barrow, 1960. Recipes and menus with descriptive introductions.

Moon, Jan. *Living with Nature in Hawaii*. Hilo, Hawaii: Petroglyph Press, 1971. Mostly about foods.

Toupin, Elizabeth Ahn. *Hawaii Cookbook & Backyard Luau*. New York: Bantam, 1967. Exotic yet easy-to-prepare dishes.